GET ME TO THE TEMPLE OF SERENITY

AND STEP ON IT!

A ROAD MAP TO PEACE OF MIND AND PROSPERITY

DAVID H. BRADY, MFA

"Get Me To The Temple of Serenity...And Step On It!" ISBN 978-1-60264-879-1 (softcover); 978-1-60264-880-7 (electronic version).

Library of Congress Number on file with publisher.

Published 2011 by Virtualbookworm.com Publishing Inc., P.O. Box 9949, College Station, TX , 77842,US. ©2011 David H. Brady, MFA. All rights reserved. No part of this publication may be reproduced, stored in a retrieval system, or transmitted in any form or by any means, electronic, mechanical, recording or otherwise, without the prior written permission of David H. Brady, MFA.

Manufactured in the United States of America.

Acknowledgements

There are a number of people whom I have to thank. First and foremost this book is dedicated to the memory of my mother. She never lost faith in me.

Throughout the years the following people have contributed to my life in a very significant way and in all honesty, I don't know how I would have made it without any of you.

All of my children, Andrew, Colleen, Brendan and Laurel. Next is my brothers and sisters, Trish, Robert, Liz and Jim. Thanks for all the help you've given me. Special thanks to Deb.

Thanks to my lifelong friends, Johnny Brower, Mike O'Shea, Alan Sacks, Brian Rogers, Jim Goodrich, Jan Haust, Mort Walsh, the late Jack Humphries, Jim Purdy, Fr. James A. Weisheipl, O.P. who inspired me to return to school, Bill Richards, Dallas Smythe and Bill Melody who guided me there.

A very special thanks to Alan Vogeler, Bob Rosenblatt, George Flak, Jack Burke, Peter Buckler, Lloyd McDonald, Dave McElroy, Dennis & Paula Kastner, Richard Landry, our late friend Bill Campbell for his wisdom and teaching us about the gift of humility in our present Master Mind group as well as Will Hodgskiss. Thanks to the guys in my original Master Mind group and especially the late Gary Sim.

Thank you to all my friends in Toronto, Los Angeles, NYC, Prince Edward County and Kingston. There are just too many to list and I'm terrified I will leave someone off, but at times I've thought of you all warmly.

Last but not least, thanks Kathy for being in my life today.

Let me also take this opportunity to say to anyone whom I may have hurt as a result of my past – I am deeply sorry and I hope you can find it in your hearts to forgive me for whatever I may have done to you.

Foreword

WE ARE ONCE AGAIN in the midst of very trying times. The late psychiatrist Scott Peck, who wrote *The Road Less Traveled*, said, "Life is hard." It was for him, and in spite of all his medical and empirical knowledge, he left this planet a broken man. According to those close to him, he was an unrecovered alcoholic with many unresolved relationship issues.

Well, if you find yourself as a result of these economic and social times feeling this way, or worse, it is my heartfelt wish that what you find within these pages will help you to find some answers. No one should ever feel shame or guilt for admitting that life is often very difficult, and we all need help from time to time to get through it. I would feel I've succeeded if anything I've written here could help you along your journey. For me, the beginning of feeling better was to change the context of trouble. It wasn't horrible—it was firming up on the downside.

I am not a behavioral scientist, although I've done graduate work in the behavioral sciences. I've worked with a number of individuals over the years dealing with alcoholism, drug addiction, adult children of alcoholics, and codependency. I have written extensively on this for various television productions as well.

I successfully confronted my own demons due to growing up in a violent, alcoholic home. I have also successfully dealt with my own alcohol and drug problems, and have lived a life free of all mood-altering substances for over a quarter of century.

I was raised in a middle-class home, and I am a successful feature film and television writer and producer. I have taught at two of Canada's universities. I am a classic over-achiever.

I have been blessed with a great deal of success, and more blessed with what I thought was crushing failure.

All of these experiences have contributed in momentous ways to my life. Out of my greatest failures have come my greatest successes. Ironically, my greatest successes have been quite empty and meaningless. I know that sounds paradoxical, but it is true. I spent the first thirty-nine years of my life pursuing material and creative success, and the next twenty-five pursuing enlightenment. I'm hoping to spend what's left of my life giving—whenever and wherever I can. It really is better to give than to receive.

This is a very odd book, quite frankly. It doesn't really fit into any specific genre. It is part self-help, part autobiographical, part observational and part inspirational (I hope). I've written it as I speak—as if I was sharing with you, one on one.

This book is about how I used various behavioral technologies and spiritual principles that are readily available to anyone to change my life and solve problems that several professionals thought were insurmountable. When I was brought to my knees in 1986, I owed $5 million and had hundreds of lawsuits launched against me from a feature film I was producing in the United States. It was at this point that I once said to a friend, " I think it's always darkest before the bottom really falls out."

I have discovered that learning can often involve pain. I have come to see that pain can be a very positive experience. If at this point you are asking, "How sick is this guy?," I don't blame you. But think about it: not only does pain tell us to go seek medical help when we don't feel well physically, it urges us to seek emotional relief when we feel overwhelmed by life and its circumstances. I am a believer in the old saying, *Religion is for those afraid of going to hell; spirituality is for those of us who've been there.*

The first chapters of this book describe my life in a general way and, I hope, will give you a glimpse of the psychological and emotional landscape on which my childhood was set. The latter half of the book is drawn from my experience working a variety of spiritual disciplines—including the eight steps of the Master Mind Principles that were developed by the late Jack Boland, a Unity minister—as well as the work I did over the years utilizing a variety of disciplines.

When I was in graduate school at Simon Fraser University in the 1970s, I attended many transformational seminars as part of my research into Communication Theory. I studied the late Dr. Gregory Bateson's Systems Theory. However, I moved on from there.

I sincerely hope that you will find value in the eight steps of the Master Mind Principle (Jack's way of stating that *when two or more are gathered, then God is there too*) and that you will find them helpful in solving whatever problems or challenges you may be facing in your own life. I want to state here that while I was raised Roman Catholic, I am not a practicing Roman Catholic, or even a traditional Christian at this point in my life. Some of you in

Canada and the United States may have seen one of my productions based on Tom Harpur's book *The Pagan Christ*, where we attempted to investigate Tom's theory that the evidence for a historical Jesus was very, very thin, to say the least. The next year I did in fact write and produce *Unmasking The Pagan Christ*, the argument for the historical Jesus that had such wonderful authors and scholars as Elaine Pagels—who made the opposite argument for the historical evidence of Christ's existence. I'm very proud of both productions. But my own beliefs are much less orthodox and much more inclusive of many other beliefs. I know there is a God, it just isn't me, and I can't put a specific name to him/her—at this point in my life. I may in the near future, but all I know and believe today is that God does exist.

But what each production showed is that there is a common bond or root to most of the world's modern religions, whether we are looking at Christianity, Judaism or Islam. They have a lot more in common than they do differences.

I cannot emphasize this point enough: you do not have to believe in any formal or traditional religion to gain benefit from what I am about to share with you. You don't have to be a Christian to have this work for you. Nor am I trying to sell you on the concepts contained in them. They were the simplest, most straightforward plans of action I could find that helped me in overcoming certain personal, financial and emotional challenges, which I faced and thought were insurmountable.

If you are looking for an empirical or dialectic discussion on whether God exists or not, then I would suggest Hans Kung's, *Does God Exist?* I only spend a brief time describing my belief and acceptance of God, as I understand God to be. I know from firsthand experience that he/she does exist. There is no doubt in my mind, and the difference between an atheist and me is that I've been where they are, but few have ever been where I am. It would take a whole different book to tackle that subject, and I know I'm not about to get even remotely close to the job Hans Kung does in describing his journey toward belief in God. You can believe in any higher power you choose, including your local hydro or power provider, and still participate in these spiritual exercises. It doesn't matter what your faith.

Chapter One
The Film That Bounced

IN AUGUST OF 1986, I was basking in the glow of three very successful and exciting film projects. First was the nomination of my then-associate Phillip Borsos's documentary film, *Nails*, for an Academy Award. Second was executive producing *Till Death Do Us Part*, a small feature film that received very favorable reviews in "Variety," The Toronto Star and from many of the critics in Canada and the United States. The HIGHLIGHT was executive producing *The Grey Fox*, an independent feature film starring the late Richard Farnsworth, presented by Francis Ford Coppola's Zoetrope Studios and released through United Artists Classics, which received worldwide critical acclaim and commercial success. T*he Grey Fox* won seven Genies, (Canadian Academy Awards) and was nominated for two Golden Globes for Best Foreign Picture and Best Actor for Richard Farnsworth. We were on a roll.

Buoyed by these successes, I began producing another feature film in the state of Washington. Originally titled *Indian Summer*, it morphed into *Dixie Lanes*. While the cast and crew were truly wonderful, the film lacked a creative and critical cohesion. I accept responsibility for those deficiencies. Previously, while I was creatively soaring, I was personally descending into a void fueled by an addiction to Bolivian Marching Powder and pot—it was akin to riding the head of an unguided ballistic missile. The trajectory was rapid, as was the descent into the dark night of the soul. However, I thought this film would be the opportunity for me to turn my life around and live "clean and sober and happily ever after," as the movies say. Wrong again. Ironically, I had not had a drink at that point since I was 22 years of age—in other words, 17 years. Clearly, just quitting drinking had not solved my problems.

This book is not about the demise of *Dixie Lanes*, my career or my finances. It is an examination of the journey upon which *Dixie Lanes* was to propel me, so I could make sense of what happened to me—why, after three previous successes over a seven-year period, did I choose a project that ended in such disaster?

The catalyst that propelled me forward was created by the problems I was having with the financing of the film. I had taken two Washington State towns and turned them back to the 1940s—then had to leave them there. The financing I was counting on and paid for never appeared in our bank account. I ended up personally owing $4 million U.S., which was over $5 million Canadian at the time, and I believed in my heart of hearts that I was going to be able to pull off a miracle, just like we had so many times before, and pay everyone off.

I thought, if I at least got the film finished, chances were I could recoup enough from it to achieve that goal. If I shut it down, there was zero chance of recovering anything, and we would be out over $1.5 million of our own money. *The Grey Fox* had run out of money. So had *Till Death Do Us Part*.

Every night, for almost three months, I would go up to my motel room, shut the door and go into a state of shock from fear. There was no one I could talk to, because everyone was counting on me to keep the picture going. Every morning before I went downstairs to start another day of shooting, I would go into the bathroom and throw up from fear. I don't know how I made it through the experience of producing *Dixie Lanes*. But over the course of three months, I went from worry, to dread, to fear, to sheer terror.

I know from personal experience what it is like to lose everything, to face massive public criticism and to face my own economic recession—and in this case, a self-created financial depression. I survived and came away more prosperous, peaceful and more purposeful than I've ever been, and I learned how to make my life manageable, keep my word and reclaim my life in spite of what appeared to be an impossible situation. In an odd way, at a micro level, my life emulated what is going on in the world today at a macro level. I had allowed greed, self-centeredness and ego (edge God out) to take over my life.

At the time, I just thought I was doing what I'd been told my father would make me successful—and, I assumed, happy. Wrong again! I hate that.

Here is what I believed, and what I had been told: make a lot of money, gain a lot of attention, acquire a beautiful home and an equally impressive car and a beautiful woman—or flip the order in whichever way you want. I had all of those things in spades. I had met several wonderful women over a seven-year period, acquired a beautiful home on the Pacific Ocean in West Vancouver, shared a beach house in Malibu with my old friend John Brower, and rented an apartment overlooking the East River in Manhattan and a beautiful town house in Toronto. I moved constantly between these four residences. Deep down, I felt that it was hard to hit a moving target, because I didn't want anyone getting too close to me. I was just reminded, on a telephone call from my friend Bob Rosenblatt about my friend Jim's yacht that he'd gotten with another friend in New York City, that I ended up living there in 1984, on Jerome Kern's old Showboat—a 74-foot yacht. So lack of material resources was not my problem. It was recklessly borrowing the money to keep that insane lifestyle up.

I find that life is often full of ironies. During that period, when I was at my lowest, I went to my old friend, the respected Canadian journalist Jim Purdy, and told him, "I feel nervous about what's happened. I expect they're going to run at me in the papers."

He laughed in his own quiet Scottish brogue and dismissed the whole notion with his hand. "You're worried about nothing," he said. "Nobody cares about you or your film."

Wrong. The very next week, the *New York Times* published an article with a large headline "The Film That Bounced." The *Seattle Times* ran an ongoing series of front-page articles for a week. In its early days, CNN covered the story. I was sitting in my apartment in Toronto when the phone rang and an associate from New York visiting Germany said, "I just saw you on CNN." At home, the story was picked up by *The Globe and Mail*, Canada's national daily newspaper.

Jim had me look at the bright side. He pointed out that you couldn't buy this kind of publicity with a million dollars. Too bad I wasn't in the market.

In addition to the $4 million U.S. that I owed personally, I had approximately 605 lawsuits launched against me. It was not just the dark night of the soul, it had moved up to bleak, barren hopelessness, and I had nowhere to turn. There is no way to adequately describe the feelings I had at that time. As mentioned previously, fear ran rampant. I couldn't sleep at night. I was filled with an impending sense of doom and a real sense of despondency. I felt totally alone. I felt abandoned. I had a sensation of sinking—like I was drowning in a sea of emotion that I had no control over. Then it dawned on me. I was either going to kill myself, or crawl out of the hole I'd dug, which originally had functioned as my shelter in my childhood to survive living in an insane alcoholic home. What had happened is that I had built an impenetrable wall around myself for self-protection, only now, as an adult, I couldn't break through the barriers I had erected to protect myself.

When I went back to Jim Purdy, he pointed out that this kind of publicity was worth its weight in gold and not to pay any attention to what the papers had written. We both laughed about it years later when I got over the humiliation of the experience. That's when I realized people were so self-obsessed that they really didn't care a week or month later what had been written about us. It was my late associate, Phillip Borsos, who was to take me off the front page when his own film, *Bethune,* was experiencing tremendous difficulties shooting in China. The headline in the *Toronto Star* read "Let them Eat Dog Meat," referring to a comment by the Chinese officials reacting to the Canadian crew's complaint about the lack of proper food.

When Phil arrived home from China, I called and thanked him for unintentionally helping me out. He was the one who suggested I should turn the negative over to the State if I couldn't come up with the money to pay the creditors.

As a result of that experience, I began to question every aspect of my life. Why did I live in a perpetual state of fear: fear of the future, fear of failure, fear of success, and fear of financial insecurity? When I had these overwhelming feelings, why did I insist on living out on the edge like I did? In my bravado, I used to say I had no fear of debt, but I was terrified of creditors.

I also wondered why, in spite of all the success I'd had, did I have such low self-esteem? I could never feel how others looked on the outside: confident, gregarious and well put together. Others saw me as a success, but I couldn't. I felt like a fraud.

No matter how well I did, my mind would tell me I could have done it better. Why did I constantly blame others for my troubles? This was not the first time I had sabotaged myself.

The moment I accepted that we were out of money on the film *Dixie Lanes* and had no hope of any, I knew my life as I'd led it was over. I also thought my career was, too. The film wasn't finished, and I was starting to think it never would be. In retrospect, I wish I'd never finished it. But that's another story.

I didn't follow the business advice I was given and declare bankruptcy. I felt if I did, I would never learn whatever it was I had to learn about managing my finances and my life. Nor would I get to the root cause of why I was out of control, financially and emotionally. If I didn't take a stand and confront myself about why I'd acted and behaved the way I had, chances were I would find myself right back in the same position again. In this case, once was enough, and I'm grateful to say it has been.

Finding the answers to why my life was so unmanageable has been a long, slow process that is still underway today. Initially, I struggled every day to stay in the game. I was incredibly depressed and wondered if I would ever be able to start overcoming any of the difficulties I was facing. I owed so much money, I didn't know where to start. Finally, after four years of very intense personal work, I began sending out payments of five dollars to various individuals that I owed thousands or hundreds of thousands of dollars to. Before that it was always just talk and empty promises. At least with five dollars, it was a real concrete action.

One lawyer in New York said I restored his faith in humanity. In the last few years the payments have risen significantly, but with so many people, I needed to generate a large amount of cash to make the final payments possible. I also had to prioritize my creditors. There is a whole group I've never even begun to repay.

I was told to take care of the people who stood by me through the difficult years first, which is where I still am today, then the trade creditors for the corporation because, while I don't have a legal obligation, I feel I have a moral one to make them as whole as I possibly can. For my original obligations, I was able to sell off certain assets I owned, such as screenplays, video rights and revenues from the film, to reduce the production debt to a more manageable level.

In addition to this book being helpful to you, the reader, it is my hope that it will accomplish two other goals: First, to allow me to personally apologize to the people of Whidbey Island and the State of Washington for any harm or pain I inflicted through my actions as producer.

My second goal is to put a minimum of 25 percent of the proceeds of this book, and any talks about how I recovered from this dilemma, toward retiring the balance of the debt from 1986, which now sits at approximately $300,000 US.

The Attorney General for the State of Washington investigated my production company. Our financial records confirmed we had paid over twenty thousand dollars to a New York law firm as the last step for satisfying all of the conditions necessary to close on the financing of the film. The New York lawyer had represented to my US lawyer and I that the money I was seeking was already on deposit, and all we had to do was pay him and our film was financed. We paid and the check was cashed, but no money ever materialized.

Live and learn. We were victims of commercial fraud.

We had another executive producer who was unable to raise all the necessary funds. But it was not for a lack of trying.

Dixie Lanes was a horrific, humiliating experience for me. I have never felt so much pain, except for my childhood, from that experience of failing. But out of pain comes growth—tremendous growth. I couldn't see it then, but in retrospect, *Dixie Lanes* gave me my life back. No one could have told me that at the time, however.

Perhaps you haven't lost millions of dollars, but you might have lost your job or your company as a result of this downturn. Maybe you are on the verge of losing your house or your car. Maybe you've found yourself with a substance abuse issue. Or, you might be facing bankruptcy, or your husband or wife or partner may be walking out on you because you have difficulty forming a long-standing relationship.

Possibly, you live in constant fear and dread about the future. You may still be reeling from the effects connected to this financial meltdown with major banks and corporations that we never believed could ever be in trouble. We lose sleep wondering about our pension funds as these companies teeter on the verge on collapse and wondering, what in God's name is going on in the world?

Perhaps you are still awestruck by the events of September 11th or the wars in Iraq and Afghanistan. How can these horrible events take place? You may be terrified for the well being of your children or your parents? You may worry that our whole society is coming apart at the seams Perhaps you have doubts about your abilities.

I know that I experienced many of these feelings and emotions, and have had the same questions racing through my mind at various times. Today, I feel as if my life has been totally changed. It doesn't mean I still don't feel angry and resentful from time to time, or I don't have bad days. However, today I am able to get back on an even keel much quicker than I ever could, and you can, too.

I am no longer powerless over alcohol, drugs or my emotions and my fears. I am no longer run by my thoughts about the future. I do have peace of mind a great deal of the time. I also have a life I could never have dreamt possible in the past. I was married for nearly twenty years, and when my wife and I split, it was done with love and compassion for both of us. I have regained the love of my son from my first marriage, and reconciled with my oldest daughter and her family. I have found the ability to forgive myself for my past mistakes. I have been able to set right those relations in my past where I hurt others—especially my family and friends.

At present, I live in a few places. First is at a small house I have on the Bay of Quinte, near Prince Edward County in Eastern Ontario. I have a nice place in Midtown Toronto. My country house is a stone's throw from the Thousand Islands, and in a short drive, I can glance across the St. Lawrence at upstate New York. I have a new relationship with a wonderful woman who lives in northern California, and Kathy and I hope to live together part of the time in Canada and part of the time in California. That's another hope for this book.

I like to sit on the deck and watch the seasons pass—each one more beautiful than the next. I am happy 80 percent of the time. I also have a mind that, when I'm in the 20 percent downturn, tells me I will always feel that way. My mind lies to me. That's why today, when my mind starts to chatter about all that is going on in the world, I just thank it for sharing.

So, how in the hell did I end up in such a mess you ask? You might say I had an unhappy childhood—only it lasted 39 years. Embarrassing to admit. But true.

Chapter Two
Timmins

TIMMINS, ONTARIO.

Today it is known as the home of Shania Twain, but in the 1950s, it was home to me and my family. The town was built on a large hill of solid rock, surrounded by thousands of square miles of rugged wilderness made up of spruce, balsam and pine trees mixed with cedar forests. A distinct, fresh, outdoor scent pervades Northern air. At night, the skies are so clear and bright you feel as if you could almost touch the stars. Often the Northern Lights shine majestically over the far-off horizon, dancing in the sky.

Timmins came into being near the turn of the twentieth century and contained the second-richest gold bearing veins in the world, outside of South Africa. The whole city was founded on mining, which is still its primary industry today.

As kids, we used to lie on our living room floor and listen to the sound of the dynamite charges being exploded thousands of feet underground. There were miles upon miles of mine tunnels running under Timmins. The explosions were created by the miners in their pursuit of the gold ore that snaked and turned endlessly in uneven patterns under the town.

From the outside, our lives looked picture perfect. We lived in a lovely house at the top of the hill on Murdock Street. My dad was a local town councilor and a businessman. We always had a nice car. My mother was very active within the community. Both my parents were staunch Roman Catholics. We never missed Mass on Sundays. Yet, beneath this veneer of socioeconomic respectability, there was a terrifying existence being lived out in silence by my mother, brothers, sisters and myself.

We were the survivors of a violent, alcoholic home. The violence was both physical and emotional. From the time I was four years old, my father would stick a 12-gauge shotgun at our heads in a drunken stupor and threaten our lives. At age 12, standing on a stairway in our nice, middle-class Cape Cod home in Timmins, Ontario, my father loaded his 12-gauge, pumped it, aimed it at my mother and me, and then pulled the trigger.

I stood frozen in fear, paralyzed, unable to move. My life was dramatically altered at that moment. Never again would I have the innocence of childhood. It was ripped from me in those seconds.

The gun jammed, and he repeated the previous steps three more times. I can still hear the metallic click of the Winchester pump firing pin as he kept trying to get the gun to fire. It was our fault, he said in a drunken slur, that he had to do this. I was witnessing and experiencing insane behavior—which, to me, was normal.

Suddenly, my older brother Robert, walked through the door. He charged up behind my dad, grabbed the gun and punched him so hard my father fell to the floor. He then bent down and grabbed my dad by the throat and started choking him, violently, smashing his head on the floor. My mother jumped on his back and started screaming, "You're going to kill him!"

He stood up and told my father, "If you ever touch either one of them again, I will kill you."

There was no doubt in my mind, or my father's, that he meant it. It was the first time in his life my brother had ever raised a hand to my dad, but there were times when he was growing up that Dad had beaten him so hard with his belt that he used to bleed. My father would walk up to him and just flail him. My brother was so afraid he'd stand there and shake.

Well, this time he was shaking from the top of his head to the tips of his shoes, but not from fear, from rage. My father lay on the floor, blood streaming out of his mouth, groaning. He held his ribs. He had hit his side on the telephone table as he fell from the punch my brother had given him. My brother just turned, looked at my mom and me, and walked out.

Shortly after, we moved away from that house, and never returned. However, the damage done never left me until I relived the experience, and erased the consequences of it from my unconscious mind. Only then did I finally put my father to rest. Living in that house was akin to being raised in an insane asylum.

But before we did pick up and leave my father for good, there were incidents and events that contributed, in both a positive and negative way, to my future psychological and emotional development—believe me, I was not without blame for a number of them.

I attended St. John's Catholic School. It was a two-storey, two-room schoolhouse at the bottom of Empire Hill. From the first day of attending school, I didn't want to be there. I was filled with trepidation and discomfort. Early on, kids realized that if they raised their hands too quickly around me, I would jump—almost out of my skin. I was precocious in an introverted sort of way, and yet incapable of focusing on my schoolwork at a very young age. Undoubtedly, I had been suffering from what is known today as post-traumatic stress, although that was totally unknown back then.

What I recall most about school is two things. First, that I felt I was stupid. Through my entire childhood, my father told me I couldn't do anything right.

So, when I went to school, I was terrified. My mind would freeze up. I would be filled with shame and guilt because I seemed to take so long understanding anything. What strikes me as very odd is how I have no real memory of my time at St. John's, Holy Family or Don Boscoe—the three elementary Catholic schools I attended. In fact, I have very few memories of my childhood—except for my closest friends. One incident stands out in my mind that had me realize, even at that young age, that I was blessed with a wonderful sense of humor. We had the Grey Nuns as our teachers. I didn't want to go to school, and I'd stayed home on the second day of school without telling my mom. I just hid until she went to work at St. Mary's Hospital, and then went back in. I knew I'd have to go the next day, but I couldn't go that day. Sure enough, the next day I went, and Sister Mary Elizabeth—I think was her name—said, "David, where were you yesterday?"

Now, remember, I'm six. My mother is a nurse, and this woman is now towering over me, about seven feet tall in my mind, with a huge black strap, which she's slapping across her hand in a very convincing way. My little brain has gone into overdrive looking for something, anything that's going to buy me time—when voila, a moment of genius. "I had to have an operation."

She was dumfounded. Her eyes bulged as she stared in disbelief. "Show me where they operated," she said.

"Oh, I can't, Sister, it's private."

So, as she's grabbing me by the ear and dragging me into the cloakroom, I'm thinking, *this is not going well.* Well, she is very upset with me, but here was a pattern that was to plague me a great deal of my life: not being honest when confronted with my own behavior. She told me that she'd called my mother at the hospital inquiring where I was. My mother had no idea, but had come home and found me there and not said anything.

I'm standing in this room, Sister is truly pissed and I can see it, and my mind is racing, and I look up and there is a flag with an elephant with big ears—it's black and green, if I remember correctly, and I said, "What's that, Sister?"

She was taken aback by my question. "It's Dumbo the Safety Elephant—it's to help you kids stay out of trouble."

I stared up at Dumbo, and out of my mouth came words that truly astounded me and proved to save my bacon that day. "Oh Dumbo, where are you now?" I said. Sister had to fight from breaking out laughing, and then she did something that astounded me. She slapped her own hand and said, "If you ever tell anyone, I will really give you the strap. Go back in there and never lie to me again." That is the point where I got that charm pays off. I didn't understand it intellectually, but viscerally, I got it.

If I have one strong memory of my childhood, it's that my next-door neighbors were really a nice family who owned the local Canadian Tire franchise, and they were incredibly kind to me as a boy. They would take me to their cottage, where I would get a break from my dad. They were so normal it amazed me and I wanted them to adopt me. I would have given anything to grow up in their family.

At school, I remember a girl named Dorothy, whom I've not talked to since I was about ten years of age, and a boy named Rory. He and I got into a terrific fight in about grade two or three...and he won.

In grade four or five, a boy from our school died when he took a bottle of Coke from a truck, the driver chased him, and he fell and cut his throat on the broken bottle. My mother and the doctors worked on him for hours, but they couldn't save him, and he died. Years later, I wondered how the driver felt. This child died for a ten-cent bottle of Coke. If I were that driver, I know I would have blamed myself for the tragedy.

What is interesting to me today is that, while I felt I was stupid, I was interested in countless subjects and hobbies. I loved to read. I loved going to movies. I loved airplanes. I loved building and engineering. I was building things like mining tunnels when I was about nine years old. I understood those tunnels needed to be shored up for support, so they wouldn't cave in. We dug down many, many feet, and braced the tunnels we created with large pieces of lumber.

For most kids, growing up in the mid to late 50s in Timmins was paradise. In the summer, the sun didn't set until late into the evening and rose very early. When I was eight or nine years old, I had to go to bed when it was still daylight out. I can still hear the songs of the robins and the cries of the nighthawks. However, I could get up and get going by six in the morning. Conversely, in the winter, it was dark by four in the afternoon. The sun wouldn't rise until nearly eight in the morning.

My summers in Timmins were spent at Gillies Lake. I was safe at the lake. There was no screaming, no fighting and no guns. I had my friends—Doug, Roy, Stan, Mark and Moe. We were like a little gang, albeit a very innocent one. We would swim from nine in the morning until late in the afternoon. I hated going home.

There was a playhouse in our backyard. It was a wonderful hideaway, with bunk beds and a trap door that led to the roof. My older brothers and sisters had used it extensively growing up, but now, as the youngest of the family, I was in possession of it and used it as a fort. And from that fort, we rained rocks down on our archenemy: the Pope gang from down the lane.

In the 1950s, rock fights were common. We would crawl around the backyard on our hands and knees, while one of us stood lookout on the roof. We would reconnoiter to see if it was safe to scurry down the lane and hurl a basket full of rocks over the hedge, and then run like hell to make sure we could get back before they rained rocks down on us in retaliation. This was a regular event, probably once or twice a week. I don't think our parents knew about our activities. I'm sure my mother didn't, because she would have taken the broom to me—which was her favorite behavioral modification tool—if she'd found out what we were doing, which she did when Moe's eye was almost knocked out by a direct hit. That was the end of our back lane 'gang' warfare. It was a good thing my mother was a nurse.

My favorite pastime in the summer with my friends was to sleep in our backyard in a tent. I think it was in 1958, when the Russians launched Sputnik. We would just lay outside and watch it orbit the earth. It was incredible to think there was a dog up there that looked something like my dog Rex. The only difference was both of its back legs worked. One of Rex's legs had been severed on my grandparent's farm, when he ran in front of the blades on the hay mower and my grandfather couldn't stop the horses in time. That's how long ago it was. Real horsepower. So there was this dog, flying around the earth in a small garbage-can-sized capsule, and it ignited our imaginations.

My friend Doug and I, and a few of our gang, went to the library and started to read about rockets. We began designing them in my backyard, then trying to construct them from pipes and various metal objects. We may have gotten gunpowder from some of our parents' shotgun shells, but I don't remember those specifics. Thank God, none of us did any serious damage to ourselves. I loved science at that point in my life. I didn't have to really study it in school. I loved everything in school, except mathematics.

The winters in Timmins were cold. I don't mean chilly, I mean cold. When you walked down the street in January, your winter boots crunched on the snow. Anyone who has ever lived in a cold climate knows the sound. In the winter, the cars all had chains on the rear tires to give them traction through the deep snow. The sound of the steel-chained tires rolling over the hard-packed snow, as they drove past our bedroom window at night, is a sound I'll never forget.

In the winter, we played hockey every day after school at the lake. I played Pee Wee for the Timmins Hotel Flyers. I remember one day when I was given the puck, and I got so excited I turned around and scored on my own unsuspecting goalie. From that episode, I inherited the name "Backward Brady." I was totally humiliated and embarrassed by that event. It was seared into my unconscious mind, and I thought I would never recover from it. That incident also dramatically affected my self-esteem, which was already subterranean from my home life and school, where I was really a classic underachiever.

But, it wasn't all bad. It was worse. There isn't a boy born in a northern climate that hasn't looked at a steel gauge fence and wondered: What would it feel like if I stuck my tongue on that fence when it's twenty below zero? (That's how cold it was in Timmins for most of the winter.) I did, and believe me, it's just like all the movies, cartoons and jokes you've ever read or heard about. It hurts! It really hurts, and honest to God, you can't get your tongue off until someone either pours warm water over it, or you rip it off—along with your top layer of skin. You only tend to do it once. Unless, of course, you're some kind of really sick weirdo. I had a lot of sick weirdo friends, by the way. They would do it more than once, believing this time, the results would be different. They weren't. That's a form of insanity very similar to drinking or taking drugs or overeating.

The other thing we loved to do in the winter was hang on the back of the local buses and ski along on our winter boots. We used to hide at night behind parked cars, and when the bus came to a stop, we'd jump out and run and hang onto the big bumpers that used to stick out about six inches from the back of the bus. It was an unbelievable thrill to slide along at twenty and thirty miles an hour. In retrospect, it was incredibly dangerous. I would be terrified today if my kids did the same thing. But, to us, it was the way to get around the snow-covered streets of our town in the winter.

———

One night when I was around eight or nine years old and my father was very drunk and angry, I remember sneaking out of the house and catching the bus as it headed down the hill. I was just going to go for a ride around the loop and head home. I just wanted to get out of the house. I was hanging on when I put my knee down on the snow. My snow pants had large leather patches that my mother had sewn on to strengthen them. Suddenly, a large boulder smashed into my kneecap, and I was in agony. I let go of the bus and tumbled off to the side of the road. I tried to stand and collapsed. I began dragging myself along the sidewalk, crying in pain. It took at least an hour to get home. My feet, face and fingers were frostbitten when I arrived at the front door. I was in serious physical and emotional distress.

When I went into the house, my dad was passed out, and I just crawled upstairs to bed. When my mother got home at midnight from the hospital, I was able to tell her what had happened. She was beside herself with worry, and she gave me a scolding I can still remember. Because of my father's alcoholism, my mother had taken a job as a nurse at St. Mary's Hospital to help pay the escalating bills my father was acquiring because of his out-of-control drinking.

As a result, there was literally no one at home most nights, except my father, who was always drunk. But it was that lack of supervision—the lack of attention to my well-being—that greatest of the issues that would plague me my whole life. I never learned to take care of myself properly. No one supervised my homework, or even checked to see if I'd done any. My older sister would come home at midnight and find me sitting up watching television. I was ten years old. I was afraid to go to sleep.

My schoolwork was a low priority. I do know that my mom, my brothers and sisters cared about me. But they were so emotionally drained from dealing with the day-to-day horror show of my father and his behavior that there wasn't much left to go around.

At home, I found it impossible to focus. We were always waiting for my father's return with a sense of dread. We never knew if he would show up drunk or sober. I can still remember the time when he got sober and stayed sober for about three months. Our lives changed dramatically. That was the first time—in fact, the only time I remember ever doing anything with him. He took me fishing at Kamaskotia Lake. It was west of Timmins and took about an hour, in those days, to drive there on an old gravel road.

What's funny is I have a perfect memory of my dad taking me out and introducing me to a famous old prospector named Mr. Jameson. He lived alone all year round in a cabin by the lake. He had no electricity and no heat, except for a wood stove. He was an interesting old man, full of incredible stories about the woods, bears and hunting. I really liked him. It was great to go fishing with my dad. We just sat there, the two of us, in quiet contemplation. My father never really spoke to me, except when he was drunk. And then it didn't make sense.

I also remember the night my father came home drunk again. He was reeking of alcohol as he stumbled through the door. He was unsteady on his feet and hanging on to the doorjamb when he saw me. He leaned over and patted me on the head. I just felt sick inside, even though he handed me two dollars, which in 1958 would have been a fortune, so I could take my friends to the local corner store.

When my father was drunk, I had two paths of escape. In the summer, I could go down to my grandparents McGale's farm near Cobalt, Ontario. Cobalt was the same town where my grandfather on my dad's side had founded his silver mine. Part of the mythology of our family had been this breaking free of the Irish poverty on my grandfather's part, and there was a lake named after us in Cobalt, as well as the mine—Brady Cross Lake Silver Mines. There was no money. But there were endless stories from my dad about how he would one day reclaim the family fortune by rediscovering a new vein—and getting the mine up and running again. I loved those stories. The fact is, in the 50s, Cobalt was losing a good portion of its population and services as many of the mines shut down. But it instilled in me a sense or hope of entitlement that one day I, too, could be counted among the wealthy, the wise, the cool, the hip that I yearned so much to be a part of. I never really recognized at a young age just how insecure I was, or how I felt like I'd been dropped into the wrong family, the wrong town, because I felt like an alien—and not one from this planet.

In the town next to Cobalt was the Haileybury School of Mining, where my father had always hoped I would go and study mining. While I dug rock, it was music, not the Canadian Shield. Haileybury was home to the original author of the Hardy Boys novels. The covers of those old books give you an indication of the geography of the town. There was a beautiful lake that stretched out for several miles, and ended bordering the Province of Quebec on the other side.

In Cobalt, I was able to roam around free as a bird. An old fence with a large gate that would swing out toward the main road surrounded the farm. When we arrived at the farm, I would jump out of my dad's car and run and open the gate.

I loved the farm. I loved the peace and tranquility of it, even as a child. For me it was as close as I could get to a mythological Shangri-La. It had no electricity, no running water and was heated with an old wood stove. I can still remember the smell of the wood stove and fresh bread baking in the morning. The house was made out of board and batten, which the weather had turned black, and was two stories high. Earth, which acted as insulation in the winter, surrounded the house and was piled up to the first-floor windowsills.

As Canadians, we have a linguistic expression we add to the ends of our sentences. Most Americans and Europeans have a field day mimicking us. It's the big "eh," pronounced 'A.' Well, when I would say it, my grandmother would say B, C, and D, and so on, until I stopped.

There was an old, creaky stairway that led up to the second floor. The bedroom walls were made out of rough cedar that had a lovely odor to it. There were old posters for various farm implements and automobiles from the 1930s and 40s tacked up on the walls. The chimney from the wood stove downstairs snaked its way through the various walls and rooms, and in winter was the primary source of heat. My grandmother had a 1911 record player that was sold by the T Eaton Company of Canada out of their catalogue. It had a standing cabinet with a top you opened upward, exposing the record and a very old stylus that held a needle that had to be replaced every time you played one of the original discs. For power, you had to turn the side crank by hand. She loved it, and I still have it today. It was stored at my friend's house in Los Angeles until a few years ago, and then I got it shipped back after almost twenty years. I had brought it to California in the mid-1980s when I'd moved there for several years. On the farm, we used to listen to it for hours. I can still remember the *Man On the Flying Trapeze*, as well as original recordings by Caruso.

My grandfather grew potatoes and hay as his main crops. He also had several horses, as well as quite a few cows and pigs. Years before, he'd run a dairy and a lumber yard, and all the equipment was still in place. It was there I learned to love the smell of a barn: the mingling of manure and hay represents one of the most comforting smells I know. I think that's is why today, I live across from a working farm. Across from the barn and just north of the house was my grandfather's machine shop. It, too, was an olfactory smorgasbord: the smell of oil, grease and gasoline mixed with old cedar walls and shakes. The ground was covered in clover that used to stick to the cuff of your pants. I could rub my fingers over my pant cuffs and smell it for weeks after I'd gotten back home. I loved that smell more than anything I can remember. We drew water from an outdoor spring that was as pure and clean as water could be. It was also incredibly cold, and it always ran, in the heat of summer or the freezing temperatures of winter.

There was an old school on the property. It was fully equipped in the 1950s, although not in use. I could not get the story straight as to who owned it or built it, but my recollection is that my granddad had built it in the early part of the 20th century to educate his kids. But that could just be wishful thinking. In fact, my mother had told me a really interesting story about her father, just before she died and about eight or nine years after I'd done a series in Canada that played on TLC called Life After Death. It was based on a bestselling book by Tom Harpur. My mother had always wanted to be a doctor, and as a teenager, she had to run away from home and move in with Catholic nuns in our hometown of Timmins, which is where she'd met my Dad at church.

When she was telling me the story, she said, "I woke up one morning at 4 or 5 am. I remember coming to and seeing my father at the end of the bed. I knew the time, because I turned and looked at the clock. I asked him what he was doing there. He just looked at me, and said, 'I'm so sorry, Vi,'"—as her name was Violet—and my mom, in a state of shock, looked back at the clock. When she turned back, he was gone. Now, she knew she wasn't dreaming because she couldn't get back to sleep, so she got up and made coffee. She was so upset. Sometime within a few hours, the telephone rang. It was news that my grandfather had died, at the moment my mother had woken up and seen him at the end of her bed. She felt that he'd come to make amends. But as a result, that old school held many found memoires for me now as an adult.

It had desks, blackboards and a large handbell that was great to ring. I would spend hours there playing school by myself. I was blessed with a great imagination, which began to expand exponentially with all of the forgotten tools of pedagogy that were present and long forgotten in that classroom.

One of the other main attractions for me at the farm was a stream that ran through the property. I discovered it when I was about 6 or 7. From then until I was about eleven years old, I would take my grandmother's washtub and float down the stream. I had great fun, and it was there that my ongoing fascination with Tom Sawyer and Huckleberry Finn would emerge. It was at the farm that my love of reading began to emerge. And it was those two books that began my journey into the world of my imagination. I was able to paint a vast mental panorama and experience emotional and visceral reaction in my mind's eye.

My grandfather was a very quiet man. He would often take me to town in his old 1940s International truck. I loved that truck and going for rides in it with him. He too had a distinct smell to him. Not unpleasant, but he had to burn some kind of material for his asthma, and it commingled with the smell of working around the farm and the barn. It's amazing to me how much smell influences our memories.

When I couldn't get away to the farm, my other escape from my father was an imaginary world up in my room. Our bedroom had a bunk bed, where my two older brothers slept. I had a little bed next to a small cupboard on the opposite side of the room. The walls were a peaceful green. Whenever it got too noisy, or there was too much screaming or violence, I would take my pillow and crawl into that cupboard. I originally thought it must have been a fairly big closet, until I went up to Timmins to revisit the house with my former wife, Deb, and our two children, Brendan and Laurel. It was part of my journey to try and put my past behind me and lay the ghosts to rest that haunted my subconscious or unconscious mind for all those years. At that point, I was in my early 40s and we'd left when I was 13—so nearly thirty years had passed.

We were pleasantly surprised when the people who had bought it from my mother almost forty years before were kind enough to show me the old bedroom. The first thing that struck me was how small the rooms actually were. They were very pretty, but small. And when I saw the cupboard, I just stood there, dumbfounded. It was no more than two feet wide. I was probably hiding in there when I was three until I was five years old.

When I outgrew the cupboard, I created my imaginary river-raft, based on my experience at the farm in the wash bucket. I sometimes wish I could muster up the memory now in my later years, but somehow it's clouded by time. What I do remember is that my imagination took me to the Deep South in the United States. From the time I had read Huckleberry Finn, the Deep South fascinated me. I loved the Mississippi River, even though I'd never really seen it, and I just knew I was going to love it the first time I saw it, which I did.

My river meandered slowly through mango trees and weeping willows, and lush vegetation covered each shore. I could hear the sound of the cicadas in the branches of the trees. I would lie on my back and imagine the sun reflecting off the canopy of translucent green leaves overhead as we slowly floated down the river—regardless of whether it was summer or winter. While growing up in Timmins, the Deep South seemed awfully appealing—especially in winter, when we were walking to school in 20 below zero weather.

I can also remember crying. I cried so hard and so long that I felt like I was going to die. I believe at one of these occasions, a pillow was put over my face to stop me. I can still remember the sensation of smothering. To this day, I cannot have anything near my face, or I go into a horrible panic. What sticks vividly in my memory is thinking, "Am I normal? Is this normal? Do other kids feel like me? Am I going insane? Am I going to die?"

I always felt like I was going to die as a child.

As I got older, my sisters and brothers began leaving home. First, my oldest sister left to go to boarding school when she was fourteen or fifteen. Then, my oldest brother Robert got married when I was about eleven or twelve. My sister Liz moved to Toronto, and then there was just my one older brother, Jim, and I at home.

I've tried to understand my brother's perspective, what it must have been like to be saddled with the responsibility of taking care of me. He was fighting his own demons about my father, too. Suffice it to say, we did not see eye to eye on anything. It was a strained relationship that did not help the situation at home. However, in his defense, if I were ever in trouble, I could always count on him to help me out of whatever trouble I was in. It was through his business connections later on that I was able to start my company and experience my first success.

I failed grade six in Timmins, the year my dad had tried to murder my mother and I. What sticks in my memory so is the shame I felt. I was twelve years old, and I had already survived, according to one therapist, the same emotional and physical violence that many people do in war zones. I had tried to explain to one of my teachers about our home life, and he wouldn't believe me, as he "knew' my father—and in his opinion, my dad was a great guy.

But, it was on August 1, 1960, shortly after the incident with the shotgun that my father, sober, loaded our luggage, and my mother and me in his Buick and started the long drive to Toronto. I have no memory whatsoever of the trip, which took over ten hours. I don't remember him ever saying he was sorry for what happened that day in the house. I can only remember seeing my first four-lane highway, the 400, and weeping willows. Like most of my childhood, it is a blank. When he dropped us off at my sister's at the top of Avenue Road Hill, I have no recollection of him leaving, although I'm sure he said goodbye. I just don't remember.

Growing up in our home exposed us to a lot of unhealthy messages. My father believed that you were nothing if you weren't financially successful. The irony is that he was always in debt and overspending. When drunk, he would go on about how much money we were going to have when he got the mine up and running again. I never tired of his optimism. It is the one gift he gave me: My sense of optimism about the future, no matter how far down I am.

My father's alcoholism robbed him of his solvency—as best we can figure it out. As it would turn out, alcoholism was to rob my father of lot more than material wealth. It cost him everything: his family, his self-respect, and his standing in the community. The paradox was that he was so well thought of by so many people. As I mentioned earlier, he was a town councilor. I've often wondered what went through his mind as he lay dying alone, and none of us came to visit him. That must have been horrible for him. But it really does bring home the point, "You reap what you sow."

I recently received an email from someone I'd known as a ten-year-old, and he referred to my dad as a real gentleman. A man who would help solve disputes in taverns and barrooms, but was a homicidal maniac at home. My father was a great guy, if you weren't related to him. He treated strangers like family and family like strangers.

I am able to recognize today how sick my father was. I can imagine how he felt, as well. I felt just like him near the end of my own drug use—beaten and in emotional agony. I honestly don't know why he was never able to stop drinking. I don't know why I was given the gift of sobriety so many years ago, and not him. Perhaps, if there is a life after death, he reached from beyond and helped me to find the strength to stay abstinent. This is how he made up to me for the pain and anguish he caused me as a boy. That's what I would like to believe.

As a young man, however, the message that *without material wealth, without success, you are a nobody*, would hound me for the next thirty years. I was driven to succeed, to be someone of prominence. It would influence whom I liked, where I lived and what I wanted out of life. Never once did I think about what might make me happy. The drive was for success and material wealth.

Chapter Three
Toronto

WE ARRIVED AT my sister's apartment at 394 Avenue Road across from De La Salle Oakland's, the Catholic School my mother had arranged for me to attend. They had also agreed to allow me to move on to the next grade. It was an impressive school, built on the crest of the Avenue Road hill, overlooking downtown Toronto. The Christian Brothers who ran and taught at the school lived in a beautiful old Victorian mansion on the property. The school itself was the archetypal early1950s architecture. Structural functionalism.

I particularly liked Brother Arthur, who would end up being my grade eight teacher. He was a very kind and gentle man, as was Brother Cornelius, who taught me grade seven. I liked Del La Salle a lot. I loved the drum corps, which in my mind was the real reason I wanted to go there. At that time, I wanted to play the drums more than anything else—but at first, I found it difficult to adjust from a small northern Ontario mining town to a large urban center.

I can still remember my first day walking down Avenue Road hill. There were six lanes of traffic. The first thing that baffled me was why anyone would call a street "Avenue Road." I always thought it was one or the other. It was absolutely astounding to me that there could be that many cars.

That August, the air was hot and humid and hung like a blanket over the city. A strange odor intrigued me. Not a bad smell, just a smell that was quite unique. I soon came to the conclusion that this smell was a trace of chlorine coming from a large swimming pool, just north of us in Eglinton Park. I began going there every day, but meeting kids proved to be harder than in Timmins.

As I wandered around the neighborhood, I was enthralled by the sights and sounds: English sports cars, which proliferated the streets of this young urban city. MGs, Austin Healeys, Triumph TR3s. My neck strained as I glanced up at 500 Avenue Road, this beautiful gray and white modern apartment building at the top of the hill, north of St. Clair. Ironically, I have an apartment across the street from it today that is a corporate apartment and edit suite when I go to the "city" from my house in the country. The old red brick Victorian houses that lined the street as I walked down the hill toward Dupont and Davenport were shaded under a canopy of hundred-year-old maples and large elm trees.

I can still remember standing in wonder at the sight of my first streetcar. The *Red Rocket*, as they were referred to, mesmerized me. Designed somewhere in the 1940s, with their rounded noses, their style and look amazed me.

These spectra of city life made me feel so sophisticated. I went into a store and picked up my first cardboard carton of milk. No bottle.

And then, I strolled east along St. Clair toward Yonge Street and came across what was to become one of my major haunts growing up. Fran's Restaurant. I'd never seen anything like it. It had square glass windows across the front section, where there were booths and several huge plate-glass windows in a semi-circle on the west side overlooking the dining room. There was a large neon sign with *Fran's* written in green, and light bulbs constantly blinking in sequence around the perimeter of it.

Every day after school at Del, I would head over to Fran's Restaurant. We always had the same thing: chips and a cherry Coke, or a toasted Danish and a cherry Coke. All of the kids from our neighborhood use to congregate there when they weren't hanging out at the old Granite Club. There were boys from Upper Canada College and Del La Salle, and the girls from Bishop Strachan, Havergal and Branksome Hall. There were also the kids from the public schools: Brown School, Deer Park and North Toronto. There was a hierarchy. Those from high school sat in the booths, while the grade-school kids, with whom I started out, had to sit on the stools, and then later on in the back. The back was created when we turned fifteen and sixteen. Old Fran thought it would be easier on him and his staff if they stuck us in a small room, which he later converted into a cocktail bar, to keep our antics from disturbing the other paying (and mature) customers, who found our behavior upsetting.

In retrospect, what amazes me was the range of interesting people who used to congregate at Fran's Restaurant.

On any given night, you would see actors like the renowned Canadian comedy team of Wayne and Schuster. Their appearances on the Ed Sullivan Show in the 1960s made them famous. Another local resident was the remarkable Glenn Gould. It seems to me that he ate at Fran's every night. We always thought he was just a bit of an oddball, with his funny hats and the scarf that he wore around his neck in winter like a perpetual British college student. Yet, he was always friendly. He would laugh at our antics, but in my memory, he was always alone. I could be wrong about that. But none of us had a clue who he was or what he was doing. His apartment was less than a block away, on St. Clair Avenue West.

On average, we would get thrown out of Fran's once a week. In the old days, they had a system where the waiter/waitress would speak into an intercom. The kitchen help was primarily Greek. Whenever the waitress would head toward the front of the restaurant, whoever was picked that week would sneak over, push the intercom button and order copious quantities of shakes, cokes and chips. It was always followed by the screams of the cook in Greek, who would come running out of the kitchen and try to catch whoever it was that had made the order.

Old Fran Deck, the owner, used to see us outside and offer us coupons that entitled us to free apple pie. He understood marketing and loyalty. Those half a dozen apple pies over five years brought him a return of forty-one years of loyalty, because I went to Fran's up until 2001, when it finally closed down. When I lived in Vancouver, Los Angeles, New York or moved back to Toronto, whenever I was back in the city, I always went back to Fran's. People could never understand my fondness for it, especially as it was beginning to wear around the edges.

My primary love in school was the Del La Salle Drum Corps. In the early 1960s, the Del La Salle Drum Corps was considered one of the best marching bands in Toronto. One afternoon I was down in the St. Clair ravine, practicing my drums. By then, we had moved from Avenue Road to another apartment at 1 Heath Street East. My mother continued to look for a house we could live in near my school. But because we were living in an apartment, I had to go to the ravine to practice my drums.

From the dead end at Heath Street East, there was a set of wooden stairs that led down the ravine to the river at the bottom of it. One of the great things Toronto's early planners did was set aside so many natural forests and parks for their citizens to enjoy. There was an occasional table set up where you could have a picnic lunch. The path was lined with felled trees and brush. In the spring and summer, I still remember the gorgeous smell as all the natural flowers and leaves began to bloom.

There were paths that ran for miles in either direction. To the north, they headed up to the Don Valley, and to the south, downtown, first under the St. Clair Viaduct, and then under the Bloor Viaduct—an enormous span bridge that carried four lanes of traffic east and west along Bloor Street. Years later, the Bloor subway line ran on a track suspended from that bridge.

The whole system was set up with walking paths and resting spots where you could sit and watch birds, or listen to the river running over rapids at certain locations. During the day, there was literally no one there. It was like my own private forest—in truth, it reminded me of my old home in Northern Ontario. It was a natural oasis in the middle of the city. I would either stand by the table or sit on it and practice my *paradiddles, flamadiddles* or *drum rolls.*

One day, as I was practicing my drums, a young fellow my age appeared and said his father wanted to speak to me. His name was Rick. He had another friend visiting him by the name of John. Rick and his parents lived in a large house where

Heath Street East ended at the ravine, where I had decided to practice.

Rick's father, a very suave and sophisticated gentleman, asked me if this was the only place where I could practice. I told him I didn't have anywhere else to go, and he conceded, "All right, then."

Rick's dad was a tall, good-looking man who drove a beautiful white Jaguar XK 140 or 150 convertible, and his mom was also very tall and very attractive. Rick had an older brother, John, and three sisters, Pat and Roz. I chummed around with them and a kid sister whose name escapes me, but she married an old friend who I haven't seen in years, Bill.

My meeting John Brower, however, was to begin the longest-running friendship I've ever had in my life. It is still going strong, forty-odd years later.

What I liked about John then was that he lived in an apartment, too. He and I were the only two kids I knew whose parents were either separated or divorced. He was very cool compared to me. He'd grown up sophisticated. His dad was a lawyer. His uncle and godfather was one of Canada's prime ministers. He had two sisters, who were really nice. I used to spend a lot of time at his apartment, and John got me interested in music. He loved music. He introduced me to R&B, and we would head downtown to the Toronto nightspots every weekend to listen to all the great bands that were around at that time. Ronnie Hawkins and the Hawks had Robbie Robertson and Levon Helm in the band. This group went on to play backup for Bob Dylan, and then went on to become The Band. Ironically, I just completed a remarkable series entitled *Yonge Street, Toronto Rock & Roll* Stories that featured John, as well as almost everyone we saw back then, from Ronnie Hawkins and Robbie Robertson from The Band to all the great musicians I'd been a fan of, including John Kay from Steppenwolf and David Clayton Thomas of Blood Sweat and Tears.

Fifty years later, I still remember holding my first party at the apartment on Heath Street East—or rather, the horror of it. I was afraid that no one would show up, that no one would enjoy himself or herself, that people would think we were hicks because we lived in an apartment and they all had beautiful homes in our neighborhood. I was so ashamed we had to live in an apartment after our beautiful house in Timmins. As it turned out, everyone had a great time. They couldn't have cared less where I lived. I was the only one consumed by those feelings of insecurity and inferiority, but they were very real to me.

Then came another black period for me. Two years after we arrived in Toronto, my mother came down with breast cancer. It was 1962. I was informed she had to go in for extensive surgery and recuperation. It was decided that I should go to boarding school in North Bay. I didn't know how I felt about that. By then, I'd stopped missing Timmins, and I was fairly well ensconced in Toronto.

Though I didn't feel like moving again, I wasn't doing very well in school. Going to boarding school felt like moving to me. However, at that point, I had never learned the basics of studying, and because of the insanity while growing up in the house with my dad, I was hopelessly behind in all the fundamentals. It was felt that the priests and the structured environment would help me get back on track.

I spent two years at Scollard Hall in North Bay.

North Bay is on the shores of Lake Nippising in Northern Ontario. Renowned as a summer vacation destination, with wonderful fishing and swimming, it also served as the railhead for the north and the west. It was built along the Canadian Shield, the granite outcroppings that form the backbone of the Province of Ontario.

It was also home to NORAD and the ICBM ballistic missile silos. It was not a great place to be in October 1962, when the Cuban Missile Crisis erupted. North Bay, the missile silos and the military air base were one of the USSR's primary targets. I can remember the priests telling us that if we heard the alarm, the air raid siren, we were to crawl under our desks or run down to the basement.

I knew lying under a desk was going to do about as much good as putting up your arm to stop a speeding car from running you down. We were glued to the radio every night as the events unfolded. We all talked about dying. I was particularly quiet on the subject. It was incredible to have lived through that period and realize that we, as a culture, came so close to annihilating ourselves from the face of the earth over pride and ego.

I remember feeling very alone. Isolated. I made a few friends that I stuck close to, and I was generally riddled with insecurity. I was not doing too well in school, just getting by. I remember meeting this tremendously good-looking girl, Sally Ann Ward, when I was 15. Sally was the highlight of that school year. I felt like a star at our school prom. God, it felt great to be liked! It was a totally innocent relationship—I never did more than kiss her good night. But it was the biggest kiss of my life. I know that my standing went way up in that school when I captured Sally's heart. She was stunningly beautiful, and about two inches taller than me. God does have a good sense of humor and does come to the rescue when we need it most. I've often wondered whatever happened to her.

The other big event that unfolded at Scollard Hall was the onset of Beatlemania. What happened was that someone brought me a copy of the Beatles' first album. I had the same haircut as they did, and I immediately fell in love with their music. I would listen to it all night on my transistor radio.

The first night I ever really got drunk was the weekend after Father Fedy called me in, sat me down and said, "We have bad news. It appears your mother is not doing too well, and she may not live. We have to figure out what to do with you. Are you all right with going home to your father?" I was terrified at this prospect.

Father Fedy was incredibly kind, but tough. I just sat there in a state of distress. Years before, when my dad had hurt me so much, I'd made a promise to myself that I would never cry again, and I couldn't cry then. I just walked out of his office in a state of numbness and went back to my room. When my roommate asked me what was going on, I said nothing. I didn't know how to open up to anyone. My mother and John Brower were the only two people I'd ever told how I felt.

Years later, I was to realize that I couldn't feel emotions other than rage, lust, fear and jealousy. That was it. I wouldn't have known an emotion if it had come up and hit me with a two-by-four. At that moment, though, I was overwhelmed with fear.

I fired a note down to John and told him I was in trouble. I couldn't express myself very well at the time. He misunderstood and sent me back a pack of pornographic pictures, which he thought was going to help me. On the envelope, he'd put: *Don't open, personal, for Dave Brady only.* Well, the priests opened them up, and the next thing you know, I'm up getting the cane. I'm thinking, "What the hell! I didn't even see the pictures and I'm getting it." I glanced over as Father whacked me, but I couldn't steal a peek. Sometimes there's no justice. God's sense of humor again.

The principal of Upper Canada College, John's school, was notified, and we both got in deep trouble. That weekend a couple of my schoolmates decided we should go out and rent a cheap hotel room and buy some booze. This would be my first drink, which would be a drunk, which would set up my pattern for drinking. I never, to the best of my knowledge, ever had a social drink.

After we'd acquired the room, we went out to the liquor store and attempted to get several individuals to buy us a bottle. No one would. Finally, a real poor-looking sot came by, and we enticed him by saying we'd buy him a bottle too. He was off like a rocket to get our hooch, and then back in a flash with the goods. We went to our room. We had a case of 24 beers and a bottle of lemon gin.

I can still remember the smell of the lemon gin to this day—it was awful. I never puked so hard in my life. But something happened to me that night. All the fears, all the insecurities, all the doubts I had disappeared, and I felt what I assumed normal must have felt like for the first time in my life. The problem was I had all the symptoms of a chronic alcoholic from my first drink. I blacked out within minutes of taking it. In other words, I was conscious, talking to everyone, having a blast, but I had no recollection whatsoever. I threw up, passed out and wet the bed, and when I came to, I thought, "Wow! I can't wait to do that again." From that moment on, I drank to change the way I felt and to stop the incessant fear. It gave me a very temporary relief from all the feelings of insecurity, anxiety and self-consciousness that had plagued me my entire life.

As it turned out, I also became incredibly obnoxious. Scollard Hall was not working out. I couldn't concentrate. I was worried sick about my mother, and I couldn't stand living that far away from her. I called my brother Jim, who came and helped me sneak away one spring morning. I hadn't yet completed grade 10 and was headed back to Toronto, but I wanted to get home and see my mother.

Chapter Four
Summer In The City

ON MY RETURN TO TORONTO, my mother enrolled me into a very small and exclusive private school, Cantab College, in Forest Hill. My schoolmates included George Eaton, whose family controlled the largest retailing empire in the British Commonwealth, and John Barron, whose family was extremely successful in the food business in Canada.

George lived on Dunvegan Road in Forest Hill. To get into his house you had to pass by a security guard, who seemed to always be on duty whenever I was there.

John Barron lived on Rosedale Heights Drive. He was always dressed impeccably. White button-down shirts, black slacks and black loafers. That was his look. He smoked Export cigarettes with no filters and kept his change in his back pocket.

At that age, all that mattered were cars and girls. I remember when John Barron got his Sunbeam Tiger. It was an English sports car with a Ford V-8. He fitted it with dual Abarth exhausts. It sounded like no other car I'd ever heard. A deep, throaty growl. He would put his foot on the gas, and the Tiger would simply sit there, wheels spinning, with smoke pouring off the pavement. We would go cruising most days after school. He too was a friend of John Brower.

Whenever I compared myself to people like George or John Barron, I was filled with shame and embarrassment because my mother had to work at Sick Kids as a nurse, while their families were so wealthy. One evening at George's home, I was going on about my dad when George quietly leaned over and said, "It doesn't matter what your father does. That's not why you're here."

It shocked me at first, but in his own way, he was saying, "Look, shut up. Nothing you say is going to impress us. We don't talk about who we are, neither should you."

Only he did it with compassion. From that moment on, I had a great deal of respect for George. He was, in my opinion, a very misunderstood and underrated human being. He had incredible insight and wisdom for his age. And when he raced cars and was referred to as the world's richest hippie, I know he was doing it to prove to himself that he had his own ability, and not just family wealth. He was also John Brower's partner in the first big rock concerts that took place in Toronto. He was involved with John in bringing John Lennon to Toronto and, it can arguably be said, the cause for the breakup of the Beatles, as it was the first time John Lennon ever played without the Beatles when he appeared with Eric Clapton, Klaus Voorman and Yoko Ono on stage at Varsity Arena in the fall of 1969. It's said that it was on Lennon's return from this concert that he told the other Beatles it was over.

However, five years before that event, sitting in George's house one night, watching one of the first color televisions I'd ever seen, we saw a show that had a new Pontiac GTO. Within weeks, it seemed,

George had one. Black with black interior. It had a 389 cubic inch engine with three two-barrel carburetors and four on the floor. The power it had was outrageous.

He took several of us out one night and drove around a traffic circle in Forest Hill so fast I thought we would crash. I lay in the back screaming, terrified because, years before, my father, drunk, had taken me in his car and we had piled up. Then my face had hit the dashboard. I was always afraid in cars, but it was also exhilarating beyond anything I had ever done. I alternated between laughing hard and screaming even louder. It was great fun!

That summer, I met Beverly Willoughby at Fran's. I was sixteen, and she was fourteen and going to Branksome Hall. I was so shy, I could hardly get up the courage to speak to her. It turned out there was competition for her affections. I had to fight a greaseball in our neighborhood on the *mean* streets of Deer Park at Yonge and St. Clair. (Those who live in the city will get the humor of that. It's like saying the means streets of Beverly Hills or midtown Manhattan. Not too mean at all.)

I actually bought my first car from this fellow—a 1953 Studebaker. It had no brakes, and I drove right into the garage door of his apartment building. He said all it needed was a little brake fluid, and I would just have to pump the brakes a few times. It did, I did, and off I went. In retrospect, I could have easily gotten myself or someone else killed. God protects drunks and fools.

On one occasion, my arch-nemesis was sitting with Bev at Fran's. I walked in, and he could clearly see I was upset. He got up, walked over and said, "Get lost. She's mine."

Naturally, I challenged him, only to find out he was one of the local tough guys. Having grown up with my older brother, who beat the crap out of me on a regular basis, I didn't think this fight could be any different. But with my brother, I didn't figure he'd really try to hurt me. This guy, he wanted to hurt me—*bad*. We stood on St. Clair, with me provoking him. Finally, when I figured he was going to punch my lights out, I kicked him straight in the testicles. He just stood there, the color draining from his face, and then he let out a blood-curdling scream and came at me. I took my high school steel-edged binder and drilled him as hard as I could across the face. Blood gushed out of his mouth and started pouring profusely down the front of his clothes, but he just got angrier. At that moment the thought was born: "Better to run today, and live to fight another day." This guy was not going down—but I was, if I stayed another second. I took off and he never caught me.

I was concerned that he would try and get back at me for the next several weeks; yet, while he lived in the neighborhood, I never saw him again. What had come out of me at that moment was a lot of unexpressed rage. I had really hurt him when my fight-or-flight reflexes had kicked in automatically, and in retrospect, I suspect my anger may have frightened him as much as it did me.

Beverly was not too impressed with my actions, but I was bound and determined to go out with her. John Brower found out she was having a party at her parents' home in Rosedale, and we made plans to crash it. It was one of the first times I resorted to drinking to get up the nerve to meet someone, and it set up a pattern for me at that young age.

I'm grateful to say I didn't make a scene at her home that night. I met her mom and dad, both of whom were really friendly and warm. Very shortly afterward, Bev's mother came down with terminal cancer, and I was at their home the night she died.

I believe Bev was only fifteen years old when her mom passed away. Her mother was a remarkably kind woman. Her dad was a very special person, too. I came to view him as the father I never had and always wished I could have.

Thank God for John Brower's grandmother that summer. She would lend John her Studebaker Grand Turismo, the car John had convinced her to buy, for weeks at a time. What a great car for an 80-year-old grandmother to be driving. It was a two-door hardtop with bucket seats and one of the first curved dashes I'd ever seen, a tachometer, and a great V-8. It was one of the best production grand touring automobiles ever made. She was like the little old lady from Pasadena, only she lived in Ottawa.

We would get dressed up in our Madras or Gant button-down white or oxford-blue shirts, our beige pants and our Bass Weejun penny loafers and go cruising. At this point we were praying to get lucky, but generally, we had no luck at all.

A number of our friends had cottages in the Muskokas. To those uninitiated, the Muskokas are arguably one of the most beautiful geographical regions of Canada. To get there, you travel two to three hours north from Toronto. Made famous by several of the Group of Seven, Canada's renowned artists from the early part of the twentieth century, the Muskokas contain pristine lakes and stunning evergreen forests.

Over the years, celebrities from all over the world have come to enjoy the stunning beauty of the lakes, the smells of the fresh pine trees and the sound of the wind rustling through the leaves on the poplar trees. I loved the quiet, the gorgeous coastlines, the smell of cedar logs in the big fireplaces that burned bright at night when the air got cool and crisp, and the call of loons on the lake at night. It is one of the most beautiful sounds in all of nature. There's magic to Muskoka.

Each cottage was bigger and more sumptuous than the next. They were truly spectacular. In the mid-sixties, Bala and Port Carling were the greatest places on earth to be, if you were a teenager—except for the beaches of California, which I would get to in 1967.

The downside for me to being there in the summer was that I couldn't understand why we had to be poor when I compared myself to the kids I knew, whose parents were captains of industry or cabinet ministers in the governing political party of the day. I wanted to live in a mansion. I wanted money more than anything else in life. I wanted to be somebody, because I really believed it was the only way I was ever going to feel all right about myself. How wrong I was!

In Toronto, Yorkville *Village* was starting to happen in the early sixties. John Brower and I would head down every Friday and Saturday night to the different clubs. We would sit and listen to John Kay's band, The Sparrows, which was to become Steppenwolf—whose big hit, *God Damn the Pusher Man,* was written by the late Hoyt Axton. Axton would star in Dixie Lanes for me twenty years later. A friend of John Brower's by the name of John Godesby played in the band. He became Goldie McJohn. We would also go down to the L'Coq Dor and listen to Ronnie Hawkins and the Hawks.

When I look back at myself back then, I have no idea why I was so insecure about my looks. I was so hard on myself. I was a good-looking kid, but I really thought I was physically ugly.

It was here that my drinking started to get out of control. John and I used to hang out at the Embassy Tavern in the Wild Night Room, where draft beer was fifteen cents a glass. On the weekends, they would bring in Fats Domino, Roy Orbinson, or other comparable acts to the Palm Grove Lounge downstairs. I can remember the first time the waiter, Garnett, allowed me to sit down and drink. He looked at me and, with his rapier-like humor, said, "Christ, are you even old enough to drive?"

I was, but that was it.

From our private school, we would head down at lunch, and I would come back to school too high to do any work.

The second hangout I frequented was the Place Pigalle on Avenue Road. It was more hip, with more university students. But I was 17 years old at this point.

My friends and I would get fairly loaded on a regular basis and go watch old WC Fields movies at the University of Toronto. I loved WC. I particularly loved his take on being an alcoholic and his references to Godfrey Daniels—his way of saying *goddammit*, which the censors would never let him do. To me, Mae West was the epitome of an independent woman. I loved her style and humor.

Those were carefree days, filled with fun and partying. Yet I was also to see firsthand the effects of drugs when one of our friends, Morley, acquired some heroin and overdosed at the Place. It was awful. It was the first time I realized that fun could get out of control. Here was a young man who seemed to have it all. Looks, money, and he lived in an incredible mansion on Dunvegan Road, up the street from George Eaton. Why had he done that to himself? I couldn't understand. But actually, I could.

My passion at that point was fast motorcycles and cars. I loved British bikes. When George Eaton got his GTO, I went to my mother and I said, "If you don't get me a motorcycle, I'm going to kill myself."

I couldn't cope with the peer pressure. My mother arranged for me to see a psychiatrist. After an hour, he brought my mother in and said, "I'd buy him a motorcycle."

Mine wasn't a cry for help. It was an acceptance that I couldn't stand the way I was feeling, and death looked preferable to me at that stage of my life. It was just so embarrassing to be poor—having no money, but being around these kids whose families were extremely wealthy.

My mother finally acquiesced, and I was able to get a motorcycle. A 1958 BSA 650. In those days, that was quite a motorcycle. In retrospect, it was odd to see me in my private school uniform, so skinny, pushing this unbelievably fast bike down the street to get it started. I had changed the pistons, so the compression was too high for me to kick it over. Once I had tried to kick it when the timing was too retarded, and it backfired and hurled me over the handlebars. I wasn't about to do that again any time soon. So, I would run down the street, jump on and put it in second gear, and away I would go. I loved the freedom of a motorcycle. I loved the speed. I loved standing out—being different. It felt good.

I have no idea how I survived on that motorcycle. Most nights I drove it drunk. My worst motorcycle accident occurred one night when I came up Avenue Road hill, flat out in fourth gear, pushing well over one hundred and sixty kilometers (a hundred miles) an hour. I had no helmet. As I came across the streetcar tracks at St. Clair, a Toronto City Roads truck was ahead, wetting down the road at Heath Street to clean it. I was too drunk to notice, and as I looked up and saw the water truck, I started to frantically try and gear down. Suddenly, my back wheels started to break out on me because of the wet road, and I had to gear up again. As I banked right into the long S turn around Upper Canada College, the bike just went out from underneath me. I can remember thinking, "Oh shit! this is going to hurt."

I let go of the handlebars and tried to jump off. It was too late. Everything started to go in slow motion. I saw the fence coming at me, and I could see the bike heading toward the fence. The trouble was, I was starting to pass the bike in midair. I don't know what happened next. I just remember hitting the wall and everything going blank, and then coming to with cars stopped and people running over to look at me. The only thing I can imagine is that I was so drunk that I was completely relaxed when I crashed, and as a result, I wasn't killed. The clutch handle had pierced the side of my finger, and I still have the scar today. The knee, which I had hit as a kid, was smashed in, but I managed to stand up. When I convinced the people who had stopped that I was okay, they left, and I crawled down Lonsdale to my house. Later, I was awakened by the sound of the police banging at our front door, but by then I was sober, and they didn't charge me with drunk driving. I explained I was in so much pain that I'd passed out. They believed me, because it was true.

You would think that experience would have been enough, but I was to repeat a similar incident six months later on a new Suzuki X6 Hustler. It was the first of the Japanese six-speeds, really fast bikes. The problem with it, as I see it today, is they hadn't perfected their frames like the British Norton, Triumph or BSAs had. The frames were made out of too light a metal, and they couldn't take the kind of riding I was doing. I came racing from Bev's, heading north on Glen Road, once again over a hundred miles an hour—and once again, I was not wearing a helmet. This time though, I had a friend on the back. When I started to bank left onto Edgar Street, the bike started to wobble. The handlebars gyrated from side to side, as did the back end. Up ahead, they were doing construction, but I didn't see the sand until it was too late. I yelled at my friend to let go. He didn't hear me, and he and I and the motorcycle smashed into a pole. Once again, I just remembered hitting the ground, bouncing and ending up in the Wellesley Hospital. My friend had surgery for several hours to take the gravel out of his face. Again, I was drunk.

My most traumatic car accident happened around the same time. We were at our friend's house, partying across from Casa Loma. We were all drinking. When we left the party, we ended up on Dunvegan Road in Forest Hill. I was without a date, and a little bored as I remember it, so I decided to liven things up and walk out onto the street. There was a large pile of leaves at the side of the road. I decided to light them on fire. My friend, who was driving, saw what I was doing and instructed me to get back in the car. I jumped in, and we peeled away, heading north and then west over to Spadina. We were going quite fast along Spadina Road when he decided to make an abrupt left turn, and we crashed into a tree. There was blood everywhere. The young woman in the front had smashed her face, and the girl beside me had fluid coming out of her ears—brain fluid. She was in very serious condition. I was able to get out of the car, and I ran to a house and started pounding on a door. Within minutes, the police and ambulances were there. The police questioned us all, but I don't really know what the outcome was.

In later years as I started to think about it, I always wondered why I didn't die or get seriously injured in one of those accidents. A mystery.

But those times were not all bad, and there were times of just plain, ordinary fun. The highlight of my teenage years was the day John Brower and I were driving our motorcycles down Avenue Road, just north of Upper Canada College. There was a black limousine with a police escort ahead of us. It pulled into the school grounds. We decided to follow it and see who it was. The driver headed around the back of the school, and then pulled up in front of the main building, just in front of the old clock tower facing Avenue Road—and to my shock, four young men crawled out: John, Paul, George and Ringo. They were changing cars so they could sneak into the King Edward Hotel. I was so stunned, all I could do was stand there. John Brower sauntered up to John Lennon and simply introduced himself, and said, "We're going to work together."

Lennon smiled and laughed. As I indicated earlier, four years later, John produced the Toronto Rock and Roll Revival with John Lennon and the Plastic Ono Band.

When John Brower decided to move to LA to go to school (and follow his girlfriend from Toronto there), I felt as if I had lost a part of myself. John would call me and describe what was happening—the weather, the cars, the girls. I wanted to get to LA more than anything on earth. Finally, after about eighteen months, he returned to Toronto.

It was at this point that I decided I didn't want to waste my life screwing up in Toronto. Like me, John Brower was committed to succeeding. We were two young teenagers with something to prove. Without saying it, we both knew that among the kids we hung out with, the only chances we were ever going to get were the ones we created.

I remember the day he had me over to his mom's when he first returned from LA in the spring of 1967. He pulled out a .45 record of this unknown band. He'd heard them at a club a few weeks before in LA. The song was *Light My Fire,* and the band was The Doors. I can remember thinking, "Wow! Is this ever good!" He looked at me and asked the question I was to ask many others: "Are you in? We can have our own record company."

Brower & Brady & Chueba Productions were born.

I went to Bev's dad and outlined my plan to him, and asked him if he would finance us. He agreed, and six weeks later, we were off to LA. We had a friend from high school who had a phenomenal voice and a great talent as a songwriter. His name was Bob McBride. John and I signed him to a management contract and jumped on an American Airlines flight to Los Angeles with him.

Chapter Five
California (Dreaming)

IN THE SUMMER OF 1967, the Sunset Strip was heaven if you were under thirty. It was American Graffiti turned upside down. Gone were the hot rods, and in were Porsches. Gone were preppy slacks, and in were bell-bottom pants with flowers. Gone was the neatly cropped and styled short hair. Our locks flowed long. Sunset Strip was beyond anything a twenty-year-old from Toronto could have imagined. It was like having twenty Yorkville Villages. We strolled past Pandora's Box, the Whiskey, Ben Franks (now Mel's on Sunset) just west of The Source, the first health food restaurant I'd ever seen, which was made famous in Woody Allen's film *Manhattan*.

At that point, John had developed an oldie album business with one of the legends of LA radio, Dick Hug, or Huggy Boy. His cohort on Big XERB out of Tijuana Mexico was Wolf Man Jack. This was long before Wolf Man's prominence in the mid- to late-70s on television. This was in the days of "Get your Wolf Man roach holder, baby." Anyone who knew his voice will remember that refrain.

We moved into a mid-range motel/residence called the Hollywood Hawaiian. It was a typical late 40s or early 50s motel residence located at the corners of Yucca and Grace, right in Hollywood. The manager was an odd fellow with large bumps protruding from his cranium. Bob McBride anointed him 'Knobby,' a name that unfortunately followed him all the months we were there.

Every week Knobby would be pounding on our door, looking for the next week's rent. In advance. Musicians! They don't have the best reputations. The motel had a pool with rooms built around it. The air was fragrant with the smell of plants, juxtaposed against the yellow hanging smog. On some days, it was so thick you couldn't see the hood of your car. In spite of that, summer in LA was gorgeous. Everything was green, and beautiful flowers bloomed everywhere.

As it turned out, the Hollywood Hawaiian was full of great musicians. Charles Lloyd was staying there. There was a young woman who kept playing beautifully, but one morning, I was so hung over I told her that if she couldn't play any better than that, she should hang up her guitar. She slammed the door in my face and basically told me to "drop dead." She went on to sell millions of albums. This was the first time in my life when I opened my mouth to change feet—in a major way.

We had brought Bob McBride down from Toronto to get him a record deal. By sheer determination, we got in to see Doovid Barskin at "Capital Records," as well as A&M records, Herb Alpert's new label. He was just beginning to be a major player. We also managed to get Bob and ourselves on the old Joe Pyne talk show. Normally Joe Pyne loved to tear people apart. It turned out he had either been from Montreal or loved Montreal, because he was just great to us.

Bob had a tremendous voice. His singing and song writing talent was remarkable. After his contract with us, he went on to be the lead singer with the

Canadian rock band Lighthouse. He sang all of their number one tunes: *One Fine Morning, Sunny Days,* etc. But in those days, Bob was out of control emotionally. He couldn't stop telephoning his girlfriend back in Toronto. Long-distance telephone calls in 1967 were not cheap. He ended up running up close to eight hundred dollars on the hotel bill. To me, that was a fortune. One night in a drunken stupor, I glanced over at him, and without warning came out of my chair and bonged him on the side of the head with a Scotch bottle. It was not a nice thing to do, but my frustration had hit the wall.

Bob also sounded more like Johnny Mathis, his hero, than Johnny did. We tried everything to meet Mathis, but to no avail. We raised private money and cut several demos. *Key on a String* is still a haunting song about children growing up with no one at home when they get there after school. Bob's empathy for people was actually quite remarkable. In retrospect, it was also incredibly insightful, and ahead of its time by decades.

Most of our time was spent at the Whisky A Go Go. On any given night, you could go in and see bands like The Righteous Brothers, The Byrds, or our heroes, The Doors. It was amazing. One night, I met Mama Cass when she was visiting someone at our motel. She was an extremely nice woman. I remember being so impressed by just how genuine and affable she seemed.

John married Michelle Finney, the young star of *Razzle Dazzle,* whose show on CBC was a tremendous hit in Canada. Her parents had taken her to LA to expand her career. One evening, Michelle introduced me to a very pretty teenage girl. As we talked, I found out her dad was Howie Horowitz. He produced Batman. I can remember being so impressed. To me, the producer of Batman was one step removed from God.

Mr. Horowitz and his daughter were very kind to this young Canadian from Toronto. I honestly don't know what happened on any of these nights, or to any of these people, because I was already starting to lose control of my drinking. I just remember thinking, "This is not good."

I would show up at a bar around the corner from our hotel, and the bartender would look at me, then at the clock, which was usually around noon, and say, "What's wrong with you, kid? Why aren't you at the beach like the others your age?"

I would just stare at him and shrug. I had already crossed over the invisible line of alcoholism: I needed to be there. It was the only way I could settle my nerves; it was the only way I could stay inside my own skin.

I was twenty years old. I was already experiencing the jitters and shakes and a very different fear. I didn't know what I was afraid of, but this unnamed fear plagued me all the time. That's how it was with me. It was as if I was terrified of failing. I felt we were in over our heads. But I was also determined that I wanted to make it. Success—it was my key to a new life. I'd be 'a somebody' if I could be successful in rock 'n' roll.

I started to miss Beverly Willoughby back in Toronto. Her dad brought her to LA, and we spent a few days showing them around and going to Disneyland. It was wonderful. Her father, Bert, was a really great man with an incredible outlook on life. He didn't believe in problems. Just challenges. When they went back to Toronto, I started to get homesick, and I didn't know what to do. By this point, my drinking was really progressing. I was into it daily, and my friendly bartender suggested I needed help. But I was not ready to admit it.

Several months later, I returned to Toronto and found out that a young musician was going out with Bev. I was quite upset and jealous, and I headed over to an apartment called the Rose Park. It was near today's St. James Town, at Bloor and Sherbourne. There, I met this folk singer, Neil. I knew his father was a well-respected Canadian journalist, but I didn't know anything about Neil. I'd seen him on one or two occasions at the River Boat Coffee House where he was playing.

I can remember sitting in the living room with him and Bev, and you could cut the tension in the air with a knife. Finally, I just got up and turned to Bev, and said, "Let's go."

I believe Neil honestly liked her. He gave her a sweater filled with colored squares that he made famous, and always wore on stage, when he formed Buffalo Springfield shortly thereafter.

We were all very innocent in those days. I'm sure, after Neil became a superstar and I bottomed out on booze at the age of 22, he really looked like the one that got away. After that night, however, I never saw him again.

Chapter Six
Married with Children

IN EARLY 1968, I married Beverly Willoughby. We moved into her dad's home in Rosedale while our mid-town flat was being renovated. That year, Bert was kind enough to allow us to get a new 1968 Volvo. In those days, the ad said, "Volvo, it lasted an average of seventy thousand miles on unpaved roads for eleven years in Sweden."

Ours lasted fourteen months before it was ready for the wrecker. In one year, as my drinking progressed, I forgot to put on the parking brake when I was drunk. As a result, it rolled backwards into the Rosedale Ravine, twice. The second time it put a huge V in the trunk where it hit a tree. It was very embarrassing, because there was only one tow truck in Toronto capable of getting the car out of the ravine. The drop was about a hundred feet or more. On the first occasion, it was sort of humorous. On the second, it was humiliating.

I would also park it on Bay Street in downtown Toronto and just leave it there when I went drinking or to work. At that time, the police didn't tow cars. They just ticketed you. I was getting fifty dollars a week in parking tickets. That was a fortune in 1968. Every month it just kept adding up. Eventually, I owed one thousand dollars in outstanding fines. Every day the police would show up at the offices of Gibson Willoughby, my father-in-law's real estate firm, and they would hand him my summonses.

After a few more accidents—where I drove through a stop sign and hit another car, and then pulled a U-turn on St. Clair on my way into the Granite Club so that another car drove right into me—my father-in-law was fed up. When I went to get the car after the last crash, the dealer just shook his head and informed me that I was not allowed to pick it up. Bert had hit the limit of his tolerance.

In many ways I owe so much to him. When first married, I was working on the floor of the Toronto Stock Exchange. He would drive me downtown via Sherbourne and Queen Street. At that corner were the local missions. He would pull his car over, and we would watch the drunks being let out in the morning, many of them sick and hung over, throwing up into garbage cans, or in the park. As we watched them, he would say, " These men weren't born here. Many of them were from good families. They were fathers, brothers, uncles and children of good, kind people. But they have a disease."

I would nod, shake my head in empathy with their plight, and not connect on any level that he was trying to let me know I was headed there if I didn't stop drinking. He was a man with incredible insight.

My brother Jim had originally obtained a position for me as a post boy on the old floor of the Toronto Stock Exchange when I was seventeen years old. Then, after a few years, I started working for a brokerage firm from Montreal. This is where I met Mike O'Shea. He was my immediate superior. He would send the orders down to me on the floor, and I would hand them to the pro trader, Bobby Dunbar. I was in the middle of doing the investment dealers' course to become a broker myself.

Every night, all of us would go out to the Savarin Tavern, the old Cork Room or the King Edward's Golliwog Room. I felt like an adult hanging out with all these older stockbrokers and traders. At this point my drinking was completely out of control, even though I was only twenty-one years old. Mike was the only other person close to my age at our firm. We had another friend, Chris Forhan, who was also trading on the floor. Together, we would get loaded most nights and end up back at O'Shea's .

My days consisted of working on the floor of the Toronto Stock Exchange and drinking at night. I was driven to earn money in the market, so I could invest in entertainment. That was my goal. But the drinking was getting in the way of my work and my plans. I would head out for a pack of cigarettes and get home two days later. For Beverly, with a newborn baby, our son Andrew, it was a nightmare. I had no idea why I was doing it, either. I just did these totally unexplainable and irrational things.

Whenever I drank, my personality underwent a tremendous change. I would go from happy-go-lucky to morose. I would become argumentative. I started dropping acid on the floor of the TSE and used to sit there just watching the tape go by, with the various symbols pulsating and shifting form, just like a handheld kaleidoscope. I was just the kind of guy you wanted handling your securities. I was like a one-man crash of 1929.

After a year of marriage, my wife Bev was on the verge of kicking me out. In March 1969, after alerting my family that I was in serious trouble, my older brother Robert came and had a talk with me. He asked, "Do you think you have a problem with drinking?"

"Robert, it's the only thing I have going for me," was my honest response.

In spite of the fact at the age of twenty-one, my hands were starting to shake every morning and I was throwing up every day, I had no idea that I was down for the count. Alcoholism is the only disease in the world that will tell you, "You don't have it." But it's no different than type-2 diabetes. Once you have it, you have it, and all you can do is arrest it. But I didn't know that then.

That's what I honestly believed. I didn't realize that I was in such serious trouble. But I was. I had become my father.

My brother suggested I needed help, and I agreed. I was not to stop drinking, however, until March 1970. It was then that I had my last drink of alcohol until this day. Forty-one years. But it was not the end of my problems. It was only the beginning. In spite of the fact that I'd stopped drinking, in spite of the fact that I'd gone for help, I was so emotionally damaged that I couldn't comprehend how sick I was. The people who helped me stop drinking were not qualified to help me deal with the pain of my past, the low self-esteem and the sense of shame that kept me in its grip, or the sense of abandonment I felt. Nothing I did would take away these feelings. I began to read in earnest, looking for the answers in psychology, theology and meditation.

I remember in early 1970 joining a group of friends and going off to a meditation retreat. My new friend Brian and I looked around at the food they'd supplied. It looked liked the feed store at the local co-op. Nuts, grains, rice, tofu. We looked at the food and at each other, and slowly made our way to the parking lot, where we jumped into my enormous Buick and raced off to the local Biggy Burger place to get a plain burger and fries. Neither Brian nor I would put anything on the burger, and people would stare at us. He like his burger burnt like shoe leather.

In those days I belonged to the millionaires' club with a group of guys who, like me, were searching for wealth and prestige but were also recovering from our drinking. I called it the millionaires' club because each of us were driving cars we couldn't afford, living in houses we couldn't afford, wondering why our lives were so unmanageable. Back then, I had a phone in the car when it really meant something to have a phone in the car. You had to talk to the radio operator to place your call.

I was never home. I was always working on some deal, which was going to be 'the one' that brought me the fame and fortune I sought. It never came, and we were always in financial difficulty.

I left the brokerage business and tried working in life insurance as part of transforming my life to a young, responsible father/husband. I did quite well and quickly progressed within the sales organization. I was utilizing motivational tapes when I heard of Earl Nightingale. For those who don't know, Earl Nightingale was a wonderful public and motivational speaker. He was brilliant. He had started franchising his work through multi-level marketing. I was excited by this man's message. It was, for me, the food of life. I talked it over with my wife and the manager of the insurance agency I was with, and we decided to start up our own company as a distributor of Nightingale's product. We formed ASK Corporation, a company selling Earl Nightingale tapes and seminars.

I loved working for myself. I was motivated. I was self-assured for the first time. I was in high gear, and I was going to set the world on fire. But there was no long-term plan in place, and I bounced from crisis to crisis.

In late 1973, after four years of marriage and the birth of my daughter, Colleen, six months before, Bev and I split up. I was devastated. I didn't know what to do. We had been together since our teens, and I was lost. Yet, we also couldn't seem to get along. At this point, it was the darkest period of my life.

For the first time in several years, my friend John Brower showed up on the scene again. One night, he and his wife invited me over to his house. "Want to try some coke?" he asked.

I told him, "I've cleaned up my act. I don't drink or do acid anymore."

He said the words that were to come back to haunt me for the next thirteen years. "Relax. This stuff's not addictive."

My first thought about snorting coke when asked if wanted to, was how did you get the can up your nose. That's how much I knew. But from the first moment I tried it, I loved it. Here was the supercharger I needed. I could stay up all night and work all day. While it was not addictive in 1973, it became very addictive in 1974.

I started to do well in business. I was now living in a luxurious apartment that I shared with another friend. It was a bachelor's dream on the fortieth floor of a new Toronto high-rise. We had a raised room that we called the playroom. There was nothing like cocaine to convince young women that sex was going to be great, because we became like supermen for the first few years. But after a few years and one too many lines, it was a large promise and poor performance. It was great in my mind. I just wanted to do more blow. "I'll be right over in a second, and this time you'll be amazed."

The parties never ended, for almost a year. I was to discover that one could spend a month's rent in a night, and have nothing to show for it but a lot of remorse.

Chapter Seven
On The Road Again

I MADE THE DECISION in 1974 to head out to the West Coast of Canada to "get my head together." I was already getting in serious financial trouble with coke. I had another relationship blow up because of my drug use. I knew I was in trouble again. The only thing I hadn't done was pick up a drink. I made a pledge to myself that I would stick a .45 in my mouth and blow my head off if I ever picked up another drink. That's how terrified I was of alcohol. I also pledged that my children would never see me drunk, as I'd seen my dad. I'm grateful to say they never have. Mike O'Shea had cleaned up his act too, and was now trying to change the direction of his life. He'd met a young woman and decided he was going to get married and settle down. I bid him and John farewell and hit the road.

I headed out of Toronto with a backpack and a change of clothes, and hit the Trans-Canada Highway. I was twenty-five years old—four years off booze, but totally screwed up. I had lost everything again. I owed money everywhere, and I didn't know where I was heading. I stopped off in Sault Ste. Marie to see my brother Robert, and then I headed west. I had never seen the prairies, and I really enjoyed the sojourn. When I got to Saskatchewan, I decided to do manual labor to try and get in physical shape. I ended up on a mixed wheat farm outside of Regina. There is nothing like the prairie sky. It is so big and expansive with sunsets that are magical: the sound of crickets, the wind rustling through the wheat fields, and the dead quiet at night.

I worked on the farm for two months. It was a good respite. I managed to save a few dollars and to really start getting physically fit. It's amazing what manual labor will do for one's mental health. I began writing daily and keeping journals of my thoughts and feelings. I started doing an inventory of my life. I wanted to work in film. I wanted to get an education. I wanted to write. I still wanted to succeed.

I was in agony over the loss of my kids, and I was riddled with guilt about leaving them. I couldn't stop thinking of them, and I would go to bed at night praying for their well-being. I've never experienced heartache the way I did then for Andrew and Colleen, yet I was a complete washout as a father. So I thought.

I was still very angry with God. I still blamed him for the pain in my life growing up. I blamed God for the physical and emotional abuse I'd taken. The idea of trusting God was too much for me, but I yearned for some kind of spiritual awakening. Somewhere in my juvenile mind, I had equated God with my father. The idea of trusting my father was totally incomprehensible to me. That is why I could never connect with the concept of God as a loving father. Yet I also wanted to connect to God, if I could.

The farm family I stayed with was traditional Christian. I believe they were United Church of Canada. As a Catholic, I can still hear my father saying, "You'll burn in hell if you ever darken the door of a Protestant church." I began attending weekly services with them, and rather enjoyed them. There was none of the formality of the Catholic Church.

I found out a few years ago that my father's brother had married a Presbyterian. His nephew from that marriage, my first cousin Tom, ironically became a Catholic priest. It seemed senseless that my father could have been that closed-minded about his own family. But he was. Those were the times, I suppose.

It does seem that nothing ever really changes. Look at the events of 9-11, where two airplanes were purposely flown into the World Trade Center, killing all on board plus several thousand people from over sixty countries around the word. All in the name of God. Poor God. He sure does take a bad rap for all the shit he doesn't do. But I digress.

I soon tired of the farm, and the yearning grew in me to keep moving. I was restless, irritable and discontented. I wanted more. I needed more.

I continued on my journey west. I went to Calgary, which in the early 1970s was a real boomtown. It was still the Wild West—at least for an easterner like myself. I loved Calgary. The Rockies off in the west left an indelible image on my memory. The city was just beginning to develop. I loved the name of the streets: The McLeod Trail conjured up images of cattle drives, even though it was now a paved four-lane road. The Bow River snaked through the heart of the city. It was very beautiful, with all the nice homes and neighborhoods that followed its route.

A new pedestrian mall had just been built downtown, and I wandered through the heart of the city trying to figure out where to live. I found a room in the southwest section of town. I had never been in a rooming house in my life. Coming from my background, it was a very interesting experience. No one knew me. No one knew where I'd come from, and no one cared. I felt liberated. I felt a new freedom in just being an ordinary person. Not a young hotshot record producer, a stock promoter or a junior wheeler-dealer. I was a young man in my mid-20s trying to find myself, like so many of my generation.

I was beginning to run low on funds. I answered an ad in a local newspaper, and found myself traveling the province selling hardware and fixtures. I was to discover that this was the business my father had been originally in. I loved to travel. I enjoyed seeing the different parts of the province.

I stayed in Alberta for a few months and decided that I really wanted to keep heading west. I was off to Vancouver. The drive through the Rockies was beyond description. No matter how many times you see the Rocky Mountains on television or in a film, nothing can prepare you for their majesty. When you drive out of Calgary heading toward Banff, the mountains begin to grow and grow, until you find yourself twisting through canyons where the peaks are stratospheric. Occasionally, I would stop just to stare at them—the magnificent ice flows and glaciers reflecting the sun off their pristine white faces, the trees so green and vibrant mixed in with the cascading waterfalls. It's at that moment that I realized what an incredible feat of engineering it must have been to build the Canadian Pacific Railway in the late 1800s through this mountainous terrain.

I arrived in Vancouver in December of 1974. It was wet and warm for December. I had picked up a hippie and his child hitchhiking outside of Hells Gate, in the Fraser Canyon. Their names were Larry and Zack. Zack would have been about two years old. Larry, like me, was in his mid to late 20s. Here I was a dyed-in-the-wool capitalist—he a true-blue socialist—and we became fast friends. The original odd couple. I was to develop relationships through him that are still in my life today, almost forty years later.

I was taken to an apartment in the West End. Vancouver was also in the middle of a development boom in the mid to late 70s. They were building high rises as fast as they could tear down the old homes. In retrospect, it is too bad. They were such beautiful old houses.

At the apartment I met Annie and Betty. They were hippies from Ontario who'd moved west years before. Initially they were skeptical of my values, and me. But I loved smoking pot, which baffled them because I wouldn't drink. I spent countless hours with them arguing in favor of capitalism over socialism. I pointed out I was a Groucho Marxist.

We lived just east of Davie Street on Nelson. Davie Street was a sociologically eclectic mix of people from the lowest to the highest. It was more like a street in New York City than Vancouver. Up near Burrard Street was sort of a sleazy, rundown section with clubs, restaurants and bars, but down at the bottom, near English Bay, it was a nice, middle-class singles neighborhood. There were grocery stores, shoe repair shops, BC Tel and restaurants. My bank was up near Burrard, and across from it was my favorite greasy spoon hangout, The Fresco Inn. It was a cafeteria-style restaurant that used to give gigantic servings of food. They had the best beef stew and French fries I ever tasted. My diet was abysmal at this point. The Fresco Inn also attracted the oddest cross section of people, depending on the time of day. During business hours it was filled with local secretaries, trades people, dentists and city workers, and in the evening, there was everything from bank tellers to transvestites. It was true diversity.

That's when Betty and Annie decided they were going to get me off junk food, even if it killed me. It was the first time in my life I started to get a little courageous with food. They lived on stir-fry and health food. It was here that I coined the term: Health food kills. I got food poisoning from bad yeast or something of that nature in one of their dishes.

During this period I returned to college, studying journalism, and then transferred to Simon Fraser University in Burnaby, British Columbia, a suburb of Vancouver. The university was built on the peak of a mountain. You literally and metaphorically had your head in the clouds.

I began my undergraduate work in communications. SFU was a tremendous place to be in the early and mid 1970s. Designed by Arthur Erickson, it was a forward-looking institution built entirely of concrete, wood and glass. There was a strange odor to it when it rained: pungent, but pleasant. It had been built in a hurry. There was an enormous open courtyard with steps at one end that led away from the university, and doors at the opposite end that led into the university. It had a large area designated for strolling and sitting, with small shops and services off on each side. There was a campus radio station where I occasionally went on the air.

Since I'd returned to school as a mature student, I discovered for the first time that I wasn't stupid. I'd believed all my life I was stupid because of what my father had told me, combined with my primary and secondary school experience. The problem had been that I never opened a book, literally from the day I started grade one until I had come out of high school. Only once did I ever study for an exam—grade 12 geography, and I read the book the night before and received 89 percent. The teacher asked me whom I had cheated from. I told him I'd actually read the book. He asked me if I would write it again, and seeing that I realized where I had made mistakes, my mark went up and he was stunned.

At SFU I was under the tutelage of several faculty members. Dr. William D. Richards had his Ph.D. from Stanford. He had studied under Gregory Bateson, whose work I've come to love. Bateson's book, *Steps to Ecology of Mind*, gave me my first glimpse into the possibility that one could empirically reconcile God, recovery from addictions and life in a systemic way. God did not exist outside of me, but was rather a part of me. Richards' work in Systems Theory enabled me to understand that we, as human beings, are too complex and interrelated to just look at the symptoms without examining the whole person and their environment.

Dr. William D. Melody was a brilliant political economist who helped with the breakup of AT&T. Dr. Dallas Smythe was a wonderful and wise man who really appreciated my eccentricities and capitalist mentality. He told me I was a capitalist with a conscience. He was a true socialist (dare I say Marxist?) and really did believe wholeheartedly in the importance of dialectic discourse. I was his and Bill Melody's teaching assistant once I was admitted to graduate school, and it was a wonderful period of growth for me.

Academia is a different world. I enjoy the people, but the politics are very baffling to me. It's a strange phenomenon that such otherwise genteel individuals operate in such a ruthless manner. I've noticed a tendency toward a hard-line need to invalidate and criticize one another's work. I recognize that it's *publish or perish*, but the developed intellect's need to prove oneself superior sets up a system of adversarial confrontation. Whether it is "defending" one's thesis or an intellectual debate, academics really go for the jugular. It's odd, since so many of them are pacifists and honestly caring of both society and the disenfranchised.

I suspect it is something in human heredity. The need to defend—to hunt, to gather, whether it is the sustenance of life or the need to have knowledge that puts one in a superior position to your adversary, neighbor, or associate. While a student at SFU, I witnessed an unbelievable demonstration of academic warfare, as several of the key faculty members from our department were discharged for trying to manipulate both faculty and students. In retrospect, it was a power struggle, where the perpetrators lost all power and found themselves out on the street. It was very interesting to watch the events unfold. I've noticed the same power struggles at every university I've ever been associated with. Generally, the right people come out on top, but not always.

At SFU, I enjoyed learning. I enjoyed that I was able to be in an environment where it was acceptable to question. I had so many questions. I loved the behavioral sciences. I was intrigued by human behavior, the human condition. It was fascinating to explore the root of our emotional evolution and intellectual advancement. It was also enlightening to question long-held beliefs about our political and economic systems.

Studying the behavioral sciences also allowed me to explore some long-held beliefs. While I recognize it is very commendable to want to help others, I suspect at the root of a good many individuals' need/desire to be of help to others serves two purposes. First, to elevate the helper in his/her own mind so that he/she enjoys a sense of moral superiority; and second, it is easier to look at others' character defects than one's own. I find it very easy to help you see where your life is in shambles, but don't ask me to look at my own.

My primary problem was that I kept seeing myself as a rebel. I always needed to be in conflict with others. I was argumentative to the point of boredom. I also hated authority and authority figures. They all were highly suspect in my opinion. I viewed them as toxic.

Larry, Annie, Betty and I headed out for the Winter Solstice to the mountains, where I was to meet two new friends, John and Millie. We drove for hours deep into the interior of British Columbia, until we came to Cache Creek, and then turned onto a secondary road. Finally, we arrived at a small mountain hamlet called Lillooet, nestled high in the mountains. It was as close to Shangri-La as I have ever seen. It is situated between the Fraser and Thompson Rivers, and amongst other things is the hottest spot in Canada in the summer. It is also a desert.

The little town itself sits high on the side of the mountains, on a plateau overlooking a large valley with the Thompson River running through it. It was a hippie's dream. There was a local RCMP detachment, but as long as you behaved yourself, didn't drive drunk and minded your own business, they didn't bother you. They were growing their own vegetables and pot. It was so strong, I hallucinated the first time I ever smoked it. I was confused because I really wanted to stop doing all drugs, but I couldn't. I didn't enjoy being out of control. I didn't enjoy always being wasted. I didn't enjoy that I was impaired and lazy once I did smoke it.

Millie and John were two very interesting people. It turned out Millie was Zack's mother, and

Larry and she had broken up, and now she was with John. Their whole community was the absolute opposite to anything I'd ever known. Their value systems, belief systems and behavior were all quite weirdly wonderful to me. Yet ironically, Millie was to become one of the closest friends I've ever had in my life.

I loved the mountains. There is a feeling that comes over me when I'm in them. My own insignificance becomes apparent to me. I envied their freedom to live in such an isolated area, so far removed from mainstream society. Everyone in Lillooet was very open and hospitable. They put us all up for the weekend. I was able to return the favor a few months later, when John and Millie came to Vancouver to attend a seminar for Arica.

One of the highlights of our weekend was when we went to a concert, which was held inside a barn. It was wonderful. The local musicians were great, the food was fabulous, and everyone had a great time. A part of me wanted to give up the pursuit of my education, and my desire to succeed, and join them. But I was on a mission. I was going to be successful. I was going to be a film and television writer, and I knew I needed an education to accomplish that. So I was off back to Vancouver that Sunday night.

John and Millie arrived in the spring of that year to do Arica, a spiritual and philosophical movement out of California. They had numbers to designate states of mind and points of view. "I want to 4000 you" meant *I want to have casual sex*. Much of my memory is faulty today, because it was so long ago. All I know is I met the most beautiful young woman there. She stood up in the room, in front of all the people, and said, "I know that Dave wants to 4000 me." Boy, was she right. She came back to my apartment on Beach Avenue that I'd acquired by now. I lived in apartment 2001, which I always thought was cosmic.

I was both excited and honored, because she was so physically and emotionally beautiful. Once again, my own insecurities had come to the forefront. But she came over to my apartment and there, I began my usual comic come-on.

I must confess one thing that I wish were true today. I was skinny growing up. As my pal Mike O'Shea used to say about me, "I was so skinny I had one stripe in my pajamas; I was so skinny I had to run around in the shower to get wet; I was so skinny that if it weren't for my Adam's apple, I wouldn't have had any shape at all." I was really, really thin.

As you can figure out, this was a bit of an issue with me. I wouldn't wear a bathing suit to the beach once I was a teenager, because I was so skinny. I would always wear long-sleeve shirts, even in the middle of summer. But here I am, buck naked, jumping around like a monkey in heat, when I bend over and pick this unbelievably gorgeous woman up and start carrying her around like a junior version of Jungle Jim—and all of a sudden my back seizes up, and I fall straight backwards and almost cripple both of us. I'm lying on the floor, I can't move. My back has seized up tighter than a drum, and she is in hysterics, thinking she's crippled me. The truth is, I went from the back seat of the car into the windshield from the accident I described earlier, and every so often my back goes out. There's nothing I can do except wait a few weeks for the pain to go away.

John and Millie, who were staying with me, came home with another friend and found this little shop of horrors, and my little 4000 blew out the door. They couldn't do anything for me, and I had to go the hospital. All they could do was throw a sheet over me and carry me sideways out the door, with one person on my feet, one on my waist and one holding my shoulders and head. And that's how they carried me into the hospital. One by one, the doctors and nurses entered the room, and I had to repeat my tale of romantic woe, while they all fought off tears of laughter. As the hours rolled by, I suppose that every nurse and young MD in the hospital wandered in to see my condition and me. And inevitably they would laugh, and say, is it really true? Near the end, I would just nod my head and dismiss them like royalty with a wave of my hand. Fortunately for me, John and Millie had a friend from the UK who was a chiropractor taking their Arica course with them. He introduced me to acupuncture, and within an hour, he had me up and walking, even though I'd felt like a pincushion an hour before.

For the next several years, I focused on my studies, interspersed with drug binges. I would develop friendships with others, but I generally stayed to a close-knit group of friends. I started driving a taxi in North Vancouver to help underwrite my costs at university. While I was there, I met several interesting people who were interested in what I was trying to accomplish. They gave me real support by ensuring I got a cab to drive on the nights I needed it. Bob was a very interesting man who had made a lot of money in the stock markets and often talked to me about my lifestyle—or lack thereof. Mike O'Shea moved out to Vancouver at this time. It was good to see an old friend from Toronto. He was now on his way to becoming a partner in a brokerage company. Web Johnson helped me start up a building maintenance company that gave my friends and me more work and more money, so we wouldn't starve while attending university.

After running the company for six months, I put an advertisement in the paper and sold the business for the next six months of billings. In 1978, this was a lot of money. I moved back into Vancouver from Burnaby, British Columbia, where I'd been living near the university. I was getting back into action.

I bought an old 1958 MGA during this period and began restoring it. Soon I was driving a very distinctive automobile—white with a red interior that everyone would point at, because it was already an antique in 1978. I loved that car. In winter, I had an old English Austin 1100, four-door sedan with front wheel drive. It was great. It burned no gas and was incredibly reliable, especially in Vancouver's climate, which was parallel to the English climate where it had been built. Not too cold, but awfully damp in the winter.

I moved to a very nice apartment on Haro Street, overlooking Stanley Park. The commute out to SFU was now taking me the better part of forty-five minutes, but I enjoyed being back in the downtown core of Vancouver, and not out in the suburbs. I started going out to the discos and ended up back in the drug crowd. I couldn't understand why—when things were so tense, when I needed to focus and pay attention—that I would find myself out partying all night. But I loved the nightlife. And Vancouver had great nightlife.

I made friends at SFU with a woman who was an avowed lesbian and feminist. However, she also lived with a very nice guy and did have a romantic relationship with him, too. I found her quite appealing and had a tremendous crush on her. I don't know if it was because she was a lesbian and seemed so unattainable, but we would go dancing and talk for hours. Like Annie and Betty, she was committed to social activism, and I was committed to capitalism. Today she is a labor lawyer. Throughout my graduate school period at SFU, we were good friends. At least, in my mind we were. She did enjoy razzing me about my beliefs, though. However, because of my relationship with Dallas, our graduate advisor, she felt compelled to try and understand what he saw in me. I began my first teaching assignment working for both Dallas and Bill Melody as their teaching assistant—the course was Political Economy of Mass Media.

During this period, I met a group of people who lived in Kitsilano. Linda Baca, who was to become my assistant and close friend; David, Jerry, Stephen, and Sonja. We also met her boyfriend, Gary, who would lose everything he had by freebasing cocaine. He went from a top earning position with a Mercedes and a sailboat to being homeless in less than five years. I've never seen such a rapid descent, outside of my own.

Kits Point in Vancouver was another great place to be in the summer. Looking across English Bay, at the West End was an enclave of hippies and laid-back artists, filmmakers and writers. It was more upscale than the West End. Fourth Avenue had health food stores and great restaurants, as did our little village off Point Grey Road. It also had nice bars where, although I wouldn't drink, I would drop in occasionally.

I was now through most of my MA coursework, and I continued working as a teaching assistant at SFU. Even though I was only a teaching assistant, it was prestigious to many people outside of academia. It helped my social life, and I was starting to really feel like I was going places. I had small business transactions closing that were providing me with ample financial resources. I got a new Peugeot. Then my old friend John Brower called me from Newport Beach, California, and said, "Come on down." He'd managed to get a beautiful house on Balboa Island in Newport Beach. I said *yes* and jumped into my new car and headed to LA. I drove non-stop for eighteen hours, and finally arrived in Orange County. What a place! I loved Newport. I loved the women. I loved the atmosphere, and I loved the drugs. I met a friend of John's, Jim Goodrich. He drove a beautiful BMW and was a world-class sailor and racer who traveled around the world in pursuit of adventures. He had the biggest bag of coke I'd ever seen. We started to party, and it went on for over two weeks.

    I couldn't believe how wasted I got there. We were out driving one night when we waved at a couple of young women in another car. A few minutes later, both were in the Jaguar XJ12 that our friend Harry was driving. Soon one was in the back with Jim and I, naked, and one was in the front with John and Harry with her blouse off, pushing her bare breasts up against the window. An old gentleman in his late 50s, probably about the age I am today, pulled up beside us, did a double-take and almost drove head-on into another car, he was so shocked.

    Suddenly, a highway patrol car pulled up beside us, flashers going, and we all panicked. We had pot, coke and mushrooms. I ate as many of the mushrooms as I could, threw the pot out the window, and John hid the coke. The highway patrol officer walked over to the car, looking backwards at his patrol car, and then spoke with his back to us. "I've checked out your Canadian plates, and there are no warrants. But I need to tell you, if I think what is going on, is going on, I want everyone in this car to get fully clothed, and I want you to go back to wherever it is you're staying. And if I see you out here again, you're all going to jail. You might behave that way in Canada, but not here. Do you understand?"

    We all replied, "Yes sir. Thanks."

    He turned slightly, smirked and walked back to his cruiser and drove away. Believe it or not, I simply said, "Thank you, God." And I meant it. I spent the rest of the night in the desert outside Palm Springs, howling at the moon—blasted on the mushrooms. It was an enchanted evening. I must confess, there were moments when I really enjoyed the insanity of those times.

Back in Vancouver, I made the decision that I wanted to really get going in business. I was getting tired of university. I wanted to start a film production company. I wanted to write for television. I wanted to be successful. I wanted to go to California. I didn't want to spend another winter in Canada, if I could help it.

Chapter Eight
Hollywood North

In 1979, while I was still in graduate school at Simon Fraser University, I acquired a beautiful house through a friend in West Vancouver. It was on a tiny street called The Dale, overlooking Tidley Cove. It was a pretty house, built on the side of a mountain, and was owned by an unfortunate young academic who was a complete jerk. I do bless him, however, because I can't afford resentment. I was living with a woman, Betty. She was a very good person who really cared about me. She wanted to get married and have kids, and I didn't. She moved out shortly thereafter.

I wrote a script for a local Canadian television series called *The Beach Combers*. The producers rejected the script, but somehow one of the editors for the show, the late Frank Irvine, got a hold of it. He called me and said, "Do you want to meet a young filmmaker who's looking for a partner?"

I said, "Yes."

The day I got the call from Phillip Borsos, I arranged to meet him and his accountant, Paul, at my house. Paul was a quiet man, very efficient and had been Phil's accountant for a few years. He was also a shareholder in Mercury Pictures and Phil's other company, Rocky Mountain Releasing. We sat down and started to talk about what Phillip was looking for and what I wanted to accomplish. He needed money, and I needed someone with production experience. It seemed like a natural match. I was good at enrolling people in projects, and he was a brilliant young director. I liked him from the moment I met him. He was incredibly bright and had a powerful vision of what he wanted to accomplish. We agreed we would meet again, and I went over to visit Phil alone, without his accountant.

He was living in a third-floor garret in the West End of Vancouver with his friend, Barry Healey. Barry had just finished directing a short .35mm film, and he was very funny, in a caustic, cynical sort of way. We would spend countless hours trashing everybody and everything—because while we were geniuses, everyone else was a moron. But it was actually done with great humor and no real malice.

Healey was writing *The Grey Fox* at that point, and Phil had a small office at 163 West Hastings, right across from Pigeon Park, as it was referred to by those on the seedier side of life. It was the beginning of skid row, filled with drunks, hookers and drug addicts, mostly heroin. Not a place I would have picked for an office, but eventually I got to like the location. It became the hub of our little enterprise that was about to spring up from a billboard on the wall of the Keg and Cleaver in Vancouver. As a young boy in Mission BC, Phil had become interested in the tale of Bill Miner.

We agreed on a formula. I was to become associate producer on *The Grey Fox*. We agreed on an amount of money that needed to be raised, and I accomplished that. For Phil, according to his friend Barry, it was if he had died and gone to heaven. All of a sudden he had money. He paid off his debts, and now he was free to develop a feature film. But there was one more problem. He needed a larger sum to pay off a production he was currently involved in, and I agreed to raise it for him. For that I would get forty percent of Mercury Pictures. Phil would have forty-five or so, and Paul would have the rest of the company.

The money was raised. That production was *Nails*. In 1980, *Nails* was nominated for an Academy Award, and it felt like we were riding the head of a ballistic missile—however unguided it was.

I moved into 163 West Hastings and merged David Brady Productions and Phoenix Pictures into the company with Phillip. Soon Peter O'Brian from Toronto, who was to become the producer of *The Grey Fox*, joined us as a partner in Mercury Pictures. Peter had successfully completed *Outrageous* and was looking for his next project.

My brother Jim agreed to help us, and introduced me to Bob Crompton and Bruce Cray. I then introduced Phillip to them. We were taken to Yorkton Securities, where Bruce Stratton agreed to finance half the film. The big question was whether Peter Brown, the president of Canarim Investments, would agree to finance the other half of the movie. His experience with films had not been good. He was incredibly reluctant, but agreed to do it anyway. In retrospect, we really owe our success to those men—Bob Crompton, Bruce Cray, Bruce Stratton, Peter Brown, and his two partners.

The feature film we started was *The Grey Fox*. In 1981, I also executive produced *Till Death Do Us Part*. It came out in 1982 to very favorable reviews.

I can't begin to put into words what it was like getting *The Grey Fox* made. It would take a book of its own to describe the unbelievably difficult time we endured getting that film finished. The tax shelter business for Canadian Feature Films was beginning to implode all around us. Pictures were shutting down one after another. Even with the strength of the people we had, our initial financing failed to close. We were in production. We had to go back and re-file our prospectus and start the whole process all over again. Every five thousand dollar unit in the film had to be pre-sold in order to acquire a firm underwriting from Peter and Bruce. Bob and Bruce Cray were able to pre-sell enough of it to gain Peter Brown's confidence again. One of the last words Peter Brown said to me was, "If you ever ask me for another dime, I'll punch you in the head."

I can remember thinking, "How much is this going to hurt?" when we had to go back to him again. I walked into his company, Canarim Investments, and he was standing by his office door. He referred to me as Diamond Jim Jr. My brother's nickname was Diamond Jim. He watched me make my way over to Bob Crompton's desk, and then we approached him. I could see the look of "Oh no, here we go again." I think I halfheartedly made a joke to him that I hoped he wouldn't hit me too hard, but we were back and needed his help because our underwriting hadn't closed. Thank God he was a real gentleman.

We persisted, pushing on, day by day. I was originally to have been associate producer so I could learn how to make a feature. Suddenly, I found myself executive producing the film and was responsible for $3.4 million. Given that I was still in graduate school, this seemed like a daunting task. But I was willing to go for it.

A few months before beginning *The Grey Fox*, I had gone to investigate EST as part of my graduate work. It was my belief that EST was a neo-fascist organization or cult that took people in and completely screwed their heads around. My friend and graduate advisor, Bill Richards, and I attended the "training."

I was stunned. It actually was a very powerful experience.

It simply utilized portions of System Theory (Buckminster Fuller, a friend of Gregory Bateson's, was also a great friend of Werner Erhard) and Zen Buddhism combined with elements of psychology. What they managed to do was illuminate how our minds run us. That is to say, I was not my mind. My mind would say, "You can't do that. You'll never make it. You'll always screw up. No one will like your idea. Who do you think you are?"

It was as if there was a rotisserie in my head that just kept spinning around with all of those negative thoughts on it. Self-defeating thoughts.

Through the training, I began to realize that my whole life was being run by messages I had acquired when I was four, five and six years of age. This is not a pitch for EST. But I do give credit to the training and the Six-Day, which I did subsequently, to giving me the ability to hang in through *The Grey Fox*, in spite of the problems we were facing on a daily basis.

Making *The Grey Fox* was an emotional roller coaster. For the better part of eighteen months, we would wake up every morning, and it would feel like we would walk out our door and everyone would take a baseball bat to our psyches and emotions. We were criticized, humiliated and laughed at. The then-head of Canada's Cultural Agency said to me, "At best, *The Grey Fox* is a mediocre effort."

I wanted to go over the table and smash his face in. The only problem was he was about six foot six and weighed two hundred plus pounds, and I was five foot ten and weighed about one forty. It's amazing what working like a maniac and the Columbian diet will do to keep you slim and trim.

Instead, I hurled verbal and emotional abuse at him, and was ejected from the Canadian Film Development Corporation's offices and told never to return. Years later I was able to make amends to the gentleman, and we both agreed we didn't really care too much for one another, but there was no reason we couldn't be civil to each other. Progress.

In the middle of all this, Phillip and I, along with Bruce Cray and Bruce Stratton, headed to Los Angeles for the 1980 Academy Awards. Phil and I were to attend, while our financial backers and friends were there for the party if we won. It was a wonderful experience. The two Bruces rented a Rolls Royce for us. As we drove up to the Dorothy Chandler Pavilion, the excitement we felt was indescribable. Walking along the red carpet with the cameras flashing and our CBC news crew following was surreal. I felt like somebody for the first time in my life. It was just amazing. When we went inside the theatre and we were shown to our seats, it was a dream-come-true moment. There were stars everywhere. We followed the ushers, who led us to the back and then up a set of stairs. When we finally arrived at our seats, we were way up in the balcony—so high you could get a nosebleed. I turned to Phil and said, "How long is it going to take you to get down there if you win?"

At that moment, we realized that just being there was our win. It turned out that the winners were all placed in the bottom rows in our category. Halfway through the ceremonies, Phil and I headed downstairs to the restaurant and ordered chocolate sundaes.

We went back into the awards show and just had a ball. Later that night, we held a party back at the Beverly Wiltshire Hotel. I don't know where they all came from, but we had about fifty people show up. It was a night to remember.

Almost two years later, when *The Grey Fox* played its first public appearance at the Telluride Film Festival, I knew my life was about to change significantly. Sitting in that darkened theatre, at the end of the film when the theatre went completely silent and then erupted in applause, screams and yelling, I knew we had a hit on our hands.

The next year, *The Grey Fox* won seven out of ten Genie Awards (Canadian Academy Awards), and we were nominated for the Golden Globes for Best Foreign Picture and Best Actor with Richard Farnsworth. United Artists Classics had released the film with the help of Fred Roos, who was then heading up Francis Ford Coppola's Zoetrope Studios. We would go on to win the Tourimo Film Festival in Italy, and the hearts and minds of critics throughout the world.

The night *The Grey Fox* opened in Vancouver was one of the biggest nights in the history of Vancouver's arts scene. Just like Hollywood, they had spotlights outside the theatre, and there was only standing room inside. Everyone was there. For all of us, for Phillip, Peter, Barry, the writer John Hunter, Richard Farnsworth and Jackie Burroughs, it was the ultimate payoff for almost three years of very hard work.

We basked in the accolades of our appreciative audience and friends. The adrenalin rush was overpowering. Yet, these feelings were very fleeting. I soon learned that success does have many fathers, and failure is an orphan. What really struck me was how unsatisfactory the whole experience was after opening night. There was no sense of accomplishment. There was no feeling of camaraderie. There was jockeying for position and praise. It actually turned quite distasteful shortly thereafter. I spoke to Phillip about it ten years after the film opened, and he was shocked to learn that it had become one of the most painful periods of my life.

In 1983, Phillip and Peter were starting *Father Christmas*, which was to become *One Magic Christmas* for Disney. I was slated to be the executive producer of that film, but I was getting restless again. My cocaine consumption was out of control. Phillip and Peter sat me down in Toronto and said they wanted me out of Mercury Pictures. In retrospect, I can't blame them.

Chapter Nine
Hollywood or Bust

I HAD ALREADY PICKED UP another project, Channel One. Everyone agreed it was a very funny idea for a film fifteen years ahead of its time. It was about how cable and public access would one day overtake traditional broadcasting. I moved to Los Angeles and acquired a very interesting house in West Hollywood. I moved into 911 North Alfred, right at Alfred and Willoughby, just east of LaCienega Boulevard.

I had made friends with Alan Sacks at the Cannes Film Festival the year of *The Grey Fox*. Alan had been an executive at ABC and had developed and executive produced *Welcome Back Kotter* and *Chico and the Man,* and was now developing feature films. I asked him if he would help us develop Channel One. He agreed. That was the beginning of a friendship that has lasted until today. Alan was brilliant in his approach to getting the most out of the script. We would work for hours by the pool, where he showed me a system for breaking down scripts that I still use today. We had a great time developing Channel One. With this project, Alan was to introduce me to several key players in Hollywood. I don't remember a time in my life when

I laughed so hard or learned so much. In 2004, I would have the privilege of being listed as one of the executive producers of Alan's Disney Channel production of "You Wish."

Bob Rosenblatt from Boston joined us in LA to help with the legal preparation, and to develop a few projects. Ironically, Bob is still working with me today, and just completed clearing all of our music rights for the *Yonge Street* Toronto Rock & Roll Stories. However, at that time we were also developing a script by a writer/director named Alan Greenberg. Alan had Keith Richards from the Rolling Stones agreeing to act as music producer. Prince, who was red-hot at the moment, had agreed to star, and Alan Greenberg had a deal lined up with the Samuel Goldwyn company to distribute the film.

Bob had introduced me to Donald Gadsden, a senior legal counsel at ABC, who, in turn, introduced us to a representative of the Saudi Royal Family. They were referred to as the Saudi Investment Group (SIG). We put together a deal for my new company, Gateway Studios, and the SIG, with me acting as executive producer and Bob and Donald as associate producers. On paper it was a great opportunity.

At the same time, we were introduced to a banker in Los Angeles named Robert Burns. He had agreed and given us written commitment to finance Channel One for $4 million US. We began in earnest to prepare the picture for production. I brought in my Toronto lawyer, George Flak, and my New York attorney, Alan Vogeler, to Los Angeles along with Bob Rosenblatt to close the financing of Channel One. Stephen Miller, who had introduced us to the man, was present too.

Mr. Burns came into the room, all smiles and chuckles, clapped his hand and said, "Do you know what we are going to do today?"

We all looked at one another somewhat perplexed, and I responded, "Close our financing, I hope."

He shook his head denoting *no*, and with an almost out of control high-pitched laugh said, "We're going treasure hunting. I'm financing the hunt for a Galleon off the coast of Florida."

He then looked to all of us for signs of approval. There was none forthcoming. Once again I had that old sinking feeling. I looked at Alan, Alan looked at George, George looked at Bob, everyone looked at me, and we all slowly turned and looked at Robert Burns. He just sat there smiling. Waiting for us to acknowledge his plan.

I turned to him. "What about our financing?"

"Oh, don't worry about that. How much do you need today?"

"Four million dollars," I replied.

"No, I mean how much do you need today, right now, to get started?"

We all looked at one another and attempted to get some more clarification. On this day alone we were probably out $20,000 in travel and lawyers fees. George sat down and did a quick calculation about pre-production financing, and we figured we could get going for about $500,000, with the balance to come within a few weeks.

"No problem," said Mr. Burns.

"Fine," I said. "Write us a check for $500,000."

He couldn't. He'd need a day or two. A day or two turned into a week, and then two. All the while I had hotel bills and lawyers' expenses building. Finally we met Mr. Burns at a hotel for lunch.

I sat across from him, and he started up again about this deal and that deal and what he was going to do. I finally blew my stack. I grabbed him by the shirt and physically held him up against a pillar in the hotel dining room. People around us were somewhat shocked. He broke down and started crying. He admitted he didn't have the funds. He'd been let go by Security Pacific Bank, and he had a little problem with reality. He just wanted people to like him.

He'd been a friend of Stephen Miller's and had done business with him in the past. We didn't know what to do. Our options were to take his house and leave him on the street. When we spoke to his wife, she was so distraught that I realized this man was mentally ill. He wasn't capable of discerning right from wrong. And then, it dawned on me just how serious the situation was. We went from optimism to bleak, barren hopelessness in the twinkling of an eye. Thus, trying to close the deal proved impossible, and to this day, the film has never been made in spite of a brilliant screenplay.

By now I had sunk close to one million dollars of my company's money into Channel One. We had to figure out a new game plan—fast! When I told Alan Sacks, he just shrugged his shoulders and said, "Hey, it's Hollywood."

Of any person to go through this exercise in futility with me, I am so grateful he was there.

Coincidentally, a director from Portland, Oregon, approached me at this time. He had received my name from someone in Vancouver and showed up at our house/office complex in West Hollywood with Hoyt Axton. Hoyt had just completed *Gremlins* for Stephen Spielberg; he'd done *Heart Like a Wheel* and *Black Stallion* for Carol Ballard. They were all pictures I liked. Here was Hoyt telling me he'd never done a movie that hadn't either been nominated for an Academy Award or made a hundred million, when a hundred million was a hundred million.

When Bob and I read the script for *Dixie Lanes,* Bob said, "Look, I may only be a lawyer, but this script doesn't seem too good."

Get Me To The Temple of Serenity... And Step on It!

His bluntness was one of Bob's most endearing qualities. I thought it was an interesting idea. More importantly, the director had someone with half the financing. I needed to start a film—given that I was now down $908,000 on Channel One, I had no immediate prospects, and the director had a reference from a producer that I really admired. When I called Peter, he said, "Yes, the director's a good lad. He has talent. He can do it."

It never dawned on me until later. Why didn't he do it, then?

A script could be fixed. We had Hoyt Axton, the man who'd written *God Damn the Pusher Man* for Steppenwolf, whose mother had written *Heartbreak Hotel* for Elvis. I saw opportunity. It wasn't. Hindsight, however, is always twenty-twenty.

The director brought in a co-producer to protect him from me. Within three weeks of starting, the co-producer strongly suggested we should replace the director. That was only the beginning of the insanity that was to follow. I wish I'd listened to the co-producer. He went from one hit to another after our film.

To go into the litany of *Dixie Lanes* is another book. I wrote another version of the story as a screenplay that I developed for a Master of Fine Arts thesis some years back. For me, though, it was a healing exercise, not a commercial undertaking.

I was to learn from *Dixie Lanes*—or rather, I was to grow to accept that I was powerless, and that my life was in serious trouble. I had been clean of drugs for six months when I started the film, but I got back into producing too soon. We ran out of money, our financing didn't close, we were being hounded on a daily basis, and we were dealing with private investors again. Every other night I was on a plane...to New York, to Toronto, to San Francisco...and by the time we completed shooting the last week of October 1986, I was running on empty. I left a few weeks before we wrapped, leaving the crew, the co-producer and the director to shut down the production, while I scrambled around New York trying to put together the last of the financing. I had no luck for six months, and the heat was building on me to find a solution. At this point, "bleak, barren hopelessness" was starting to look good to me as I descended into fear, terror, sheer terror, and then complete hopelessness.

Once again, George Flak came through and was able to arrange close to three quarter of a million dollars in post-production financing. It was based on the successes I'd had with *Grey Fox* and *Till Death Do Us Part*. We were put through the meat grinder in Seattle trying to satisfy all the creditors. Time and time again, the whole project came within seconds of collapsing. There was so much distrust swirling around the production. Finally, through the help of another law firm in Seattle, which Alan Vogeler arranged, George Flak and the Seattle lawyer were able to negotiate a deal with our creditors. The Attorney General and our co-producer agreed to have the negative moved to Canada to complete postproduction. If it were to sit in Seattle, it was unlikely anything would have ever happened with it, because the negative was a lightning rod for litigation.

I returned to Toronto to finish the film. Already, nearly six hundred people were suing me, and the Attorney General for the state of Washington was investigating me. It was the longest year of my life, and it only got worse day by day.

At this juncture, I met the woman I would end up marrying. It turned out that Deb thought I was a complete flake. I pursued her for months on end, while she rejected every advance I made. Unfortunately for her, "No" was simply an enticement to me. That's all I'd ever heard in life, and I never actually took NO to mean NO from anyone. It just meant *no, not now* to me. Finally she acquiesced and went out with me. Our first date was one of my screenings of *Dixie Lanes*. She hated it. But she didn't know how to tell me. She asked a friend of both of us what she should do. Sue said, "Lie, if you like him."

I had fallen head over heels in love with her. Besides my children, she is the best thing that has ever happened to me, and I am so grateful I had her in my life for twenty years. We moved in together and set up house.

In the midst of the post-production of *Dixie Lanes*, I'd started to want to go back up to Timmins and see if I could trace the roots of my maladaptive behavior.

For Deb, it was her first trip with me. Unfortunately for her, there were no exotic locations, but here she was, six months pregnant, in a Pontiac Grand Am roaring off to Timmins. It was about five hundred miles straight north from Toronto. First we went and looked at the house I grew up in. We drove to a hotel and stayed for the night. I spoke to one friend from my past, but he didn't want to see me. His wife had just died, and he wasn't seeing anyone. I felt very sad. However, I knew I had to face the horror of my childhood and begin healing the past to stop it from haunting me.

Almost ten years later, we would go back up, and this time I was able to go through the whole house with the people who bought it almost forty years ago. That was when I did put the ghosts of my past in their place.

My second trip with Deb was to the LA Film Market in the spring of 1988. Here, I finally recognized that the only good thing that could be said about *Dixie Lanes* was that it was in focus and that the sprocket holes were in the right place. With this revelation, I curled up in the fetal position in The Good Night Inn on the 101 North of LA and wished I could disappear.

At the screening were several hundred of my creditors, cast and crew, as well as buyers. As the movie ended, there was a riotous reaction from the audience, who were just grateful I'd finished the film and now saw a possibility of getting their money back. Several buyers were clearly mystified. While the film didn't appear to be very good to them, we would be paid a significant amount of money for ancillary rights, such as video, because of the audience's reaction. Unfortunately, the video company never recovered their initial investment and soon went out of business.

Deb cared for and nurtured me through that bout of ontological implosion. One minute I was strolling down the street, brimming with self-confidence, the next filled with fear and paranoia. I had the emotional stability of nitroglycerine at that point in my life.

Dixie Lanes was my Waterloo. At the premiere in Milan, Rona Wallace, an old friend who had been the vice president of MGM Video when I rented her home in Beverly Hills, came to the screening. She fell asleep on my shoulder twenty minutes into the film. Even I knew this was not a good sign. I remember heading back to my hotel in Milan, looking out the window and thinking, "I should jump." Trouble is, with my luck at that point, I would have ended up paralyzed and helpless, and not dead. We were heading out the next day for Venice, and the thought crossed my mind, "Death in Venice: Part two."

When I returned to Toronto from Europe, it was the start of the hardest period I had faced until then. I didn't get a night's sleep for over a year.

Every day, people called me and threatened to sue me. Eventually I became immune to threats. I remember a creditor from Los Angeles calling and starting to scream, and I quietly said, "You have two choices: you can stop screaming and talk calmly, and I will listen, or I will hang up."

He blared back, "Well, you listen to me, you motherfucking scumbbag, I'm going to sue you. How do you like that?"

I quietly said, "Take a number. I believe you are 604. Good luck."

I calmly hung up the phone, and a few hours later he called back. "You weren't kidding, were you?"

"No, I wasn't," I responded. "Would you like to work with me? Because if you are, I'm willing to try and get you some, or part, or all of the money. I just don't know how right now."

My poor bride Deborah sat in a state of shock as the obstreperous calls kept coming in. Every day I woke up, and, inch by inch, I felt as if I was dying. I was at a loss about what to do. I was completely defeated. I'd skated on thin ice through my entire career. I'd been very cavalier in the way I'd done business, and on every other occasion, it had worked out. Not this time.

It makes me realize in retrospect that character building is never an easy process, and when given the option between character building and having a good time, character building gets left in the dust of self-serving enjoyment.

I don't know too many people who wake up one morning and say, "I feel good today. I think I'll go out and subject myself to some very serious emotional and mental shit-kicking so I can grow as a human being."

Yet everyday, in every city on earth, people wake up and have to confront what isn't working in their lives. They have marriages that are in crisis, kids who hate them, bills they can't pay, jobs they hate, or jobs they're losing. They may have family members or loved ones who are sick or dying.

They have doubts about their sanity and doubts about their abilities. They feel like frauds, failures and screw-ups. In their minds, there is no hope, no ability to solve the problems they are facing, and they don't see any future for themselves. They succumb to suicide or a slower form of self-destruction through drug addiction, alcoholism, food addiction, sexual addiction, gambling, stealing, lying and cheating, with the misguided hope that these activities and actions will allow them to feel better for a while. It may only last a few minutes, a few hours or a few days, but at least it will change the way they *feel*.

None of us choose our parents, but we choose how we react to them. None of us are responsible for how our parents acted or reacted to us growing up. Most of us are making decisions about our lives from the point of view of a three to twelve year old—except for those fortunate few that seem to be totally well adjusted and mature. And they are out there. You may be one of them. Perhaps what I am about to embark on will help you understand the friend or family member who doesn't think like you.

That is my hope. The next section of this book will outline to you exactly how I came to change my beliefs, my attitudes and my way of life.

I have a life today that is good. Is it perfect? No. But it's a lot better than it ever was. No longer am I plagued by fear all the time. I don't lie awake at night worrying about my future the way I once did. I don't beat myself up constantly for making mistakes. Generally, today, you can count on me to do what I say I will do. Am I perfect? No, but there has been marked and significant improvement.

Today, I believe I am worthy. I do deserve to have a happy and peace-filled life. I believe it's all right to have sufficient material and financial resources to live comfortably. I believe there are enough resources in the world for everyone. I do believe in sustainable growth–emotionally, intellectually and financially. I believe that we can turn our lives around and have supportive, loving and happy relationships. I believe we can save our planet. We can have peace on earth.

I have to stay vigilant, however, because I have a mind that lies to me. My mind has a toxic dwarf up there (think the movie Lord of the Rings—it's his evil twin brother) belittling me when I don't feel like I've accomplished very much. It tells me, "You loser. You'll never change. She'll blow you off."

Today I thank the toxic little bugger and say, "Thanks for sharing. Now just piss off."

How did I get here, you ask? By taking the first step.

Chapter Ten
A New Way of Life
I Surrender—Step One

> *I surrender. I admit that, of myself, I am powerless to solve my problems, powerless to improve my life. I need help.*

THERE ARE MANY WAYS to enlightenment. One can walk, run, drive or fly. No matter which mode of transportation you choose, they will all eventually get you to the same place. That's why today, I've stopped judging people and organizations that teach or guide one to a better way of life. I don't believe any religion, philosophy, or movement of any kind has the market cornered on gaining insight into human behavior.

One spiritual plan I did run across—which is just about the simplest but most effective path—was that of the late Jack Boland and his eight steps to *Master Mind Consciousness*. Once again, this is not a pitch for his church, which is still strong in Detroit, Michigan. I never personally met the man, but I did get to know him. Through his writings, his audiotapes and through my interaction with some friends when we decided to follow his Master Mind Principles, which I still do today—almost twelve years after I found them. Jack was also a fellow traveler. A recovered alcoholic, he knew and understood defeat and surrender. He knew pain intimately. The pain of loss, of rejection and failure. Yet he turned his life around and became a Unity minister. I love the work of another one of Unity's ministers, Catherine Ponder. I have read and will continue to read on a daily basis her book, *Open Your Mind to Prosperity,* for over twenty-five years.

Many years ago I sent Catherine Ponder a note, and she was kind enough to respond. My question had to do with free will and surrendering my beliefs about free will, God and prosperity. I am often torn by guilt. It's not okay for me to have wealth. It's not okay to want to have a sailboat, a nice car, and a nice home for my family when so many people are starving or doing without. I couldn't bring myself to reconcile how it is okay for us in the west to be consuming so many of the world's natural resources, while thousands of children die because of hunger.

We are so wealthy, even our poor often live like kings compared to the poor in the countries of Africa or the Middle East. The Palestinians live in groveling poverty, and their leaders drive around in Mercedes. It's not right. But I am powerless over their situation. I am powerless over how they live their lives or how they choose to die. But I can have compassion. I can share a portion of what I do have with them. I can give away a portion of what I earn and let everyone and anyone prosper from my own resources. I can find a practical way to make a difference.

During my time in New York, I lived in a penthouse apartment overlooking the East River on Sutton Place at 53rd. Prior to that, I'd been staying at the River Towers on 53rd. In addition, I would also spend a lot of time on the yacht of my friend from California, Jim, which was berthed under the Brooklyn Bridge next to the River Café and the old World's Fair Marina in Queens. He and another woman had bought Jerome Kern's 'Showboat.' It was the sister ship to the presidential yacht. It was over 70 feet long, had a commercial kitchen, several major staterooms, plus numerous guest quarters and a beautiful living room. It was a floating mansion.

I stayed on that yacht for months on end. During Christmas of 1985, Jim left me alone while he went skiing in Vermont. I don't know why, but instead of staying in the spacious stateroom, I stayed up in the crew's quarters near the bow of the boat. During that time, I freebased a lot of cocaine by myself. I kept a propane torch going twenty-four hours a day, for three days straight.

While I was there, a terrible cold snap hit. All Jim had asked me to do was check the generator's oil level to ensure it was full. However, in my insanity I forgot. The generator ran out of oil, and the engine seized. As a result, the furnace stopped working, and the whole yacht froze up, except for the cramped quarters I was in. A constantly burning propane torch heated that. The hot water pipes all burst, and when Jim returned from his ski weekend, I was still sitting up in the crew's quarters with my pipe and torch, not realizing how much damage I had caused. Unfortunately, that wasn't enough to stop me from freebasing cocaine.

Every few months I would return to my office in Vancouver for a few weeks to catch up on business. I had a staff and a partner who handled the administration of our company. We were in the process of going public. The paperwork was significant. At the same time, we were developing several movie and television projects.

On one trip home, I was invited to Miami for a

weekend. I drove my car to Seattle and took a direct flight from there. I was going to see Leo, whom I'd met at the Telluride Film Festival the year before. Leo was a certified public accountant and had many business holdings in the United States. He was interested in investing in our company, and I went to speak to him about it. As it turned out, he was also significantly involved in the drug world. I really wanted to do a film about cocaine. I had already produced my first film, *Alcohol, Drugs and the Young*, as part of my coursework while I was doing my MA in communications.

When I arrived in Miami, I was taken to a beautiful guest condominium. I then went to Leo's home, which was in South Miami. I met his lawyer and accountant, Howard. He was your typical lawyer and accountant, except for two features. When I sat down in his Corvette, my ass banged up against something hard. I put my hand down and pulled out a .44 Magnum. He assured me everyone had one in his or her car in Florida. Given my history with guns, I was not too impressed. As it turned out, Howard was also an addict of the first order. So much for stereotyping people.

Leo's compound was beautiful. He'd brought in his contractor from Colorado and completely redone the house and property. Later on, I would end up staying at the compound in the guest quarters. He had three or four Jaguar XJ 12s, a Porsche Turbo and another Jaguar. He had a lot of cars, and he had his own mechanic. He introduced me to a bevy of beautiful women. Leo knew how to entertain. He was also one of the first people I ever met who was really into developing personal computers. He was just rather unorthodox in his approach to business. He too eventually straightened out his life, and today lives an exemplary life. But not back then.

We began to talk about feature films and what was involved in financing them. When I discovered he had copious quantities of cocaine hidden around the property and was friends with Columbian coke dealers, I spoke to him about doing a film on that world. He set it up so I could meet some of them.

My weekend trip turned into a five-month sojourn into hell. Miami was the worst experience of my life. It was a nonstop nightmare of debauchery—although I must confess that there were some times I will remember with fondness until the day I die.

We made the secret film of the Columbian coke dealers that I wanted to use as a behind-the-scenes documentary of the drug world, but I ended up getting caught up in the insanity of it myself. I believe I consumed over a kilo of cocaine. Why I didn't die, I will never know. I remember going to the hardware store to buy more propane tanks to smoke the freebased coke, and the clerk asking me what I was doing with them. I said, "I'm stripping a boat." On about my 20th visit in a few weeks, he said, "What's the boat? The Queen Mary?"

On one particularly harrowing run, I watched as a Columbian coke dealer's Doberman attacked his own newborn baby and punctured its cranium with its teeth. In spite of the screams and protestations of his wife, the dealer was unable to destroy the dog, because he cared more about it than his own child. That's when I realized I'd better get out of there if I wanted to live. I was told that it was rumored that this man had walked up to a car at an intersection, stuck a shotgun through a car window and blown his adversary in two for not paying his debts. These were very, very scary people. The tape was turned over to a former US Federal Agent for safekeeping at Leo's insistence. I have no idea where it is today.

I was not in good shape at this point. I was falling hopelessly behind in organizing any new productions, and my life was starting to completely careen out of control.

I returned to my new apartment in New York City. Gone was the penthouse, and now I was in a more bohemian neighborhood downtown. It was there that I began my last cocaine binge, which was to go on for a month straight. Near the end, a fellow I'd met came over to my apartment one night and asked me if I wanted to get high. I said, "Sure." We called my dealer, and he came over. Five hours later I was calling my old friend Jim for help. The fellow had overdosed. Jim called an ambulance. They revived him in the hospital, but he died of an aneurysm a few days later. That was the last straw for me.

On Holy Thursday—the day before Good Friday, according to the Catholic tradition in which I was raised— of 1987, I stood in Washington Square Park in New York City. I had wandered over from my apartment at Lafayette and Spring to score some dope. In those days, Washington Square Park was like a drug supermarket. You could get whatever you wanted. I bought some pot. It was crap. I went back to the dealer and said, "You just sold me shit."

He looked at me with a sneer. "Fuck off."

I was so insane, I grabbed him by the arm. "Give me back my money," I screamed at him.

He fired back, "Look, asshole, people like you get shot."

I got right in his face. " Then shoot me, because you aren't getting out of here without giving me back my money."

Now, I want to clear up a few misconceptions about myself, in case you think I'm some kind of tough guy. I weighed maybe one hundred and forty five pounds. I was totally insane. I was beyond desperate, because I wasn't able to raise the money yet to finish *Dixie Lanes* and I had started using again after almost a year off everything. I was trying to come down off the cocaine. I was totally, clinically and absolutely insane. I had no fear of dying. I had a real fear of living. I was a very scary person, and my friend in the park got it. I wasn't some dipshit coming downtown to score. I was a very spooky addict.

He threw my money back at me. I wandered over to another dealer I knew and bought another bag of weed.

I turned and walked out of the park over to Sixth Avenue. I stood on the corner of Sixth and Waverly, looking at the old apartment of my former girlfriend, Jo. I was filled with regret and sorrow.

To this day, I still do not know what happened, but here's how it unfolded. I stood looking uptown at Sixth Avenue. A voice inside of me that was as clear as a bell said, "You'll die if you start on that bag of dope."

Without knowing why, I threw it in a garbage can and started walking uptown. I crossed over to Fifth Avenue. My mind was racing. I couldn't think straight. I just knew I needed help. What I find mystical, and somewhat peculiar, is at that moment in Toronto, a very old friend of mine, Jack Humphrey, lay in his house in Rosedale, dying. Jack and I had stopped drinking at the same time seventeen years before. We had remained good friends, and it was Jack who told me I could be the funniest writer in Canada. He was producing such Canadian series as *King of Kensington, Hanging In* and *Flappers,* and had just started executive producing *Silver Spoons* for NBC, when he was diagnosed with lung cancer.

When Jack came to California, he would call me, and I would go over to the Beverly Hills Hotel and have lunch with him and tell him my woes. He was always patient, kind and supportive. He never lost faith in me, even when I didn't have any in myself. When I found out he'd died at approximately the same time I threw the drugs away, it sent a chill down my spine.

I was thinking I would go talk to my lawyer, Alan Vogeler. It was a long walk uptown to Rockefeller Plaza. I kept reflecting on the mess I'd made of my life, the relations I'd harmed, my children and my mother. I looked up, and I was standing outside St. Patrick's Cathedral. I walked inside, found a pew and sat down. I dropped to my knees, tears streamed down my face, and I cried out, "If there is a God, please help me."

People close to me looked over, and I could see the uncomfortable looks on their faces and in their body language. I didn't care. I covered my face with my hands and just sat there, totally drained. I've often wondered, if I weren't so well dressed, whether they would have let me stay there.

I left St. Patrick's and walked across Fifth Avenue to Rockefeller Plaza and up to Alan's office. I went in and told him I was in serious trouble. He thanked me for my candor and asked me what I was going to do. I told him I was going to try and get clean.

I called a new friend of mine, Linda, and headed up to her apartment. We'd met months before on a wet Friday night in Manhattan, when we both tried to hail the same cab. In New York, little old ladies have been known to assault very large men in order to hold onto 'their' cab. She was a real diplomat and said, "Why don't we share this taxi?" After that, we had become friends and even enjoyed a brief romantic relationship, but I was too fragile when I met her and not available. At least I had been honest with her, and as a result, we had remained friends.

I called her and she told me to come over. She was going out of town for the weekend, but told me to make myself at home. I explained that I couldn't go back to my apartment. It was a dangerous place for me, because my coke dealer would inevitably show up with a bag of it and call me with the words, "I'm downstairs." I was always powerless to say no to him, and it would send me off again on another binge. I never returned to that apartment. I just left all the furniture, my clothes, carpets, stereos and personal belongings, because I knew I would fail if I went back. I had to be willing to go to any lengths to get clean.

I crawled into bed and started to shake and sweat, coming off the blow and the pot, cold turkey. I know in retrospect I should have been in a treatment center. But I didn't go.

On Friday morning, Linda got up, checked on me and made me coffee and toast. Everyone who knows me will laugh at this recognition. I lived on toast and cereal. Long before Seinfeld made an issue of it, I survived on that combination. I was unbelievably shaky. I felt sick to my stomach. Pain shot through every limb, joint and muscle in my body. My head hurt, my hair hurt. I just put one foot in front of the other. I had a yearning to go to Good Friday services. Linda was Jewish, but agreed to go with me to keep me company before she left town.

It was very cold that April 18th. There was a brisk wind blowing along West End Avenue that chilled me to the bone. I had never bothered to get myself a proper New York or East Coast winter coat. I had a Barney's trench coat, which I wore all winter. I froze—but I looked good. It was always important to me to look good. I inherited that trait from my father, too.

We went to a small Catholic church on the Upper West Side. As I sat contemplating my life, I was overcome with a sense that I had surrendered. There was no more fight left in me. My need for terminal uniqueness was lifted right out of me that morning. At that moment, I yearned for normalcy. I just wanted to stop hating myself, and to forgive myself for having destroyed so many wonderful opportunities.

I surrendered my ego to the idea of God, because I couldn't figure out who or what God was. I have come to accept that when my ego is in full force, it is hard for me to connect on any spiritual level. EGO= Edge God Out. My ego was responsible for my inability to accept my powerlessness over drugs. My ego kept me locked into self destructive, self-sabotaging behavior. It had been useful as a child when I needed it to survive: to reinforce that I was okay and deserved to live. But now it had turned on me. It was dangerous to my survival. Often people confuse humility with humiliation. They are not the same. Often humiliation can lead to humility, but not always. I had to let go of a lot of beliefs in that small church. I needed God more than God needed me. I needed help in the worst way.

We returned to Linda's apartment, and she prepared to leave town for Easter weekend. She had Shirley MacLaine's tape, *Out On a Limb*, which I'd never seen. I sat and watched in a state of bewilderment. I didn't necessarily subscribe to any of her beliefs at that time, but I must confess, right then, I was grateful to see that show. I put it back in the machine and played it over several times that weekend. What was important to me was the message: when I try and run my life, I end up in serious trouble.

I have to surrender and believe in something outside (or inside) of me. It is imperative if we are to find happiness that we come to see that there is a

Power greater than we are. At this stage of my life I really was agnostic. I wanted to believe, but all my education, all my experiences in life told me it was wishful thinking. It would be nice if there were a God and an afterlife, but the fact was, I believed that all that happened after we died was that a part of us survived in our children. That's what I believed that day. Yet I knew I had to believe in something. As I stated earlier, God could be as simple as *Good Orderly Direction.*

Two years later I was sitting and talking to my friend, Tim McCauley, and his friend, John Heard, who starred in *Out on a Limb*. I told him how much the show had helped me. He laughed and shared how he was in a dark place himself when he'd made it. He was going through his own 'dark night of the soul' in the area of relationships. It hadn't really registered at that level with him, but it's interesting to see how he did work that he never knew would end up possibly helping to save another human being's life.

Later that year, George Flak invited me to a luncheon at the Bel Air Hotel in Los Angeles for Canada's former Prime Minister, Pierre Trudeau. I was able share with his escort, Shirley MacLaine, how much I'd been helped by the show. I always thought that those two events were tied in to the miracle of my recovery.

But back in New York that Easter weekend, I was in desperate shape. I knew I wanted to get better. I knew I had to go back out to California, where I was sharing a house in Malibu with my old friend John Brower. I was terrified that he and I would start partying, and that would be the end of my sobriety.

I crawled onto the plane a week later and flew back to LA. It was early May. I had just met with George Flak and his friend, Nick Stiliadis, and they agreed to fund the completion of *Dixie Lanes*. We would release it as an SC Entertainment Picture. In that regard, I felt like a thousand-pound weight had been lifted off my shoulders. At least now I could get the film finished, and hopefully pay off all of my creditors and get my life to a place I'd never been: sane and clean.

When I arrived at the airport, John picked me up. He and I had shared apartments and houses in LA for years. I would pick up part of the rent so I would have a place to stay when I arrived in town. First was the Hollywood Hawaiian, all those years ago with Bob McBride. Then there had been an apartment in West Hollywood, and then a gorgeous house in Beverly Hills, on North Beverly Glenn Drive. Now we had a great beach house on Old Malibu Road. When I told him that I had to stop using drugs, he just looked at me and said, "Thank God. I was worried about having to talk to you." He had come to the same realization while I had been in New York.

In the insanity of our last party the month before, we had driven in and out of East LA at 10:00 pm, then 11:30 pm, then 1:00 am, then 2:30 am, then 4:00 am—the only two white guys in a white LeBaron convertible with the top down, looking to score crack in Watts. No fear for our lives. No fear of driving into an area that was not exactly conducive to a healthy lifestyle for two thirty-year-old guys from Malibu.

On our last jaunt, an LAPD helicopter hovered over us as we were trying to score. The bull horn squelched and a voice said, "What are you doing down there?"

I looked up and yelled, "Canadian tourists. We're lost."

They must have believed us, because seconds later a black-and-white pulled up beside us and motioned for us to follow him. Within moments we were on the Santa Monica Freeway heading west, back to Malibu. We still had the coke, which we hadn't thrown out. Now talk about insanity. It was only through the grace of God that I was never arrested and put in jail. It's certainly not because I didn't deserve it.

Years later when I was doing our series on counter-terrorism, I said to a US agent, "Can I make amends to you?"

He looked at me rather perplexed. "What kind of an amend?"

I explained to him that years ago I had little regard for law enforcement, or their rules, and that I had often thought ill of them, and I wanted to use him as a person I could express my sincere regret for the way I'd acted and thought. He was very touched. I also felt a lot better, and today I've made friends with a number of individuals within the law enforcement community. I've acquired a tremendous amount of respect for them and the job they have to do. A part of me wishes that I could go back and change the way I was in my twenties and early thirties. But I can't, and I've had to accept that.

Our local neighbors in Malibu thought we were a couple of wild and crazy guys, as Steve Martin used to say. John was a sports addict. In the spring, there would be multiple televisions going. On one or two would be the Stanley Cup playoffs, and on the others would be the various basketball playoffs. We were hanging out with a great group of people, including my friend Jack. I was attending mass regularly at Our Lady of Malibu. I love that name. For non-Catholics, they break out in laughter. But for us, it is as normal as sunshine. I was also hanging out with people like myself that were interested in staying sober. That was healthy for me.

I was torn about going back to Toronto. While my family and my kids from my first marriage were there, the city had a lot of bad memories for me. But if I wanted to finish *Dixie Lanes*, I had to return. I created a plan of action. I would call some old friends that I knew I could trust. I would tell them the truth about what kind of shape I was in, and I would surrender to their direction. I would trust these people because I couldn't trust myself, or God, quite yet. I wanted to, but I just couldn't. It was in April 1987 when a young lady I was seeing in Malibu gave me a copy of Catherine Ponder's book, *Open Your Mind to Prosperity*.

At this point, I still believed that money would solve my problems. I kept thinking it was the millions I owed that was the deep, underlying issue. It was not. However, the book contained a series of prayers that gave me comfort. They enabled me to come to believe that I was worthy, and that I could have what I needed, and I began to see that prosperity meant a lot more than just money.

This was a completely new concept for me. I never thought of spiritual prosperity where I had enough...enough money to live on for that day, enough food to eat for that day, enough love from my wife and children to do me that day. We had a home. I had friends who truly loved me when I couldn't love myself. I had friends who were willing to go to any lengths to support me, as long as I was going to put the effort in to changing my way of life and my way of thinking.

Change is not easy. It can be very painful. It is frightening. We need to acknowledge ourselves for taking the risk to change. For many of us, our behavior is something we learned as children that supported us when we were young. It is how many of us survived. To give up that behavior and head into untried territory is bedlam. I felt nervous and excited about returning to Toronto. It had been years since I'd left, and I had no idea what to expect.

John Brower had arranged with a friend of his for me to sub-lease her apartment at Bay and Bloor. It was a very central location, and it turned out that one of my oldest friends lived in the same building. His friends referred to him to as the spiritual giant. He was someone I could trust and count on for guidance. He and my old friend Brian helped me get back on my feet. It was with this friend who, along with Brian, I'd gone on the meditation retreat seventeen years before.

He had also been doing some work on himself, and had come across a workbook about "Adult Children of Alcoholics." He also had an alcoholic father who was abusive. Like me, he also had to deal with shame. We attended an information meeting and decided to take the workshop. That decision was one of the turning points in my life. I had to start looking at my powerlessness in a number of areas besides substances. I had to look at how I was powerless over relationships, my need to control, my need to be overly critical and judgmental. I was powerless over perfectionism. No one would be able to do it as well as me, so therefore I had to do it all. Of course, I would soon become angry and resentful at anyone I was in a relationship with, or working with, because I had to do it all.

The best example of what I am talking about is the insanity of getting on an airplane, of which I have a fundamental knowledge of how they fly, yet having the need to go up and make sure that the pilot's doing it right. How in the hell would I know what right is, if I've never been trained? But I sure wanted to go up there and check it out. My friends and I attended these writing workshops for twenty-six weeks. It was extremely powerful and extremely painful at times, and finally, it was extremely liberating.

So, surrender took on many meanings to me. First, it was that I was powerless over alcohol and drugs; next, I was powerless over my finances and my career. I was powerless over unhealthy relationships—I would continue to go to people who were incapable of giving me what I needed. I was powerless over what my children from my first marriage thought of me, or what my ex-wife thought of me. I was powerless over the thoughts that came into my mind about what I had done in my life. But I was not powerless over what I did with those thoughts, if I got help.

I had to temporarily surrender my business and my goals so I could re-contextualize my life. I needed a new set of values, because obviously my old ones weren't working. The therapist I was seeing, Dr. Rose, pointed out to me that I needed a complete overhaul in the way I viewed life and success.

I went to my two oldest children, Andrew and Colleen. I remember it as if it was yesterday. I met them at their mother's home in Leaside. We went upstairs, and I sat them both down. I explained that I'd been completely out of touch with reality. I acknowledged that I'd developed a very serious drug dependency. I then confirmed for them their own feelings that I'd left them high and dry when I'd moved out to Vancouver. I didn't get into the reasons why. I just said, "I know I let you down." I apologized for my past behavior and asked them if they could forgive me. I asked them if there was anything they needed to say to me.

My son, who is very quiet, looked at me for a moment, and then with incredible clarity and force simply said, "I don't trust you. You've lied to us time and time again. I have felt hurt my whole life for what you did. But I'm willing to give you one more chance."

As he went down his list of my character defects, it felt like a knife going through my heart. All of a sudden, I was really aware of how much I'd hurt him. He couldn't understand why I'd left Toronto. Somehow, I think he felt he was partly responsible for my actions. I assured him he wasn't. It was solely my choice, and had nothing to do with him per se. I just needed a change at that point in my life. I was in too much pain to stay in Toronto.

My daughter said that she didn't think of me as her father, really. I'd left when she was a baby. So to her, I was like a long-lost relative who'd pop in from time to time and visit. She always enjoyed the visits, but she said she didn't really have any outstanding issues. It would turn out a few years later, that those issues would finally surface, and today, we have found a way to resolve them.

Clearing up the wreckage of our pasts is not an easy task. It is painful and it is slow. But it must be done, if we are to receive any peace of mind. It is well worth the price of admission to get back on a healthy footing with those we love.

When I returned to Dr. Rose, he pointed out I also had to change my priorities. As an example, when I was in serious financial difficulty and several months behind on our rent, I was offered a position with the Canadian Broadcasting Corporation's *Newsworld*. This was a new Canadian news service like CNN, only with a Canadian perspective. I love news. It's why I had studied it first in college. When I went to him full of excitement, he simply looked at me and said, "Find a new therapist if you take that job."

I was devastated. I couldn't understand why he was saying this to me when I needed money so desperately. I'd gone to my friend George Flak to get the job in the first place. "Why?" I demanded out loud.

"Because you need to work on yourself."

He pointed out that, in his opinion, I would probably die if I went right back into a pressure-cooker situation. I had too recently recovered from my drug addiction. If I really wanted to get better, I had to follow his lead and begin examining my life in its minutiae. I had to work on my life before I worked for a living.

"Here we go again," was my initial reaction. I just thought it was all BS. My mind went insane with anger.

"Nobody understands me." I started to get unhinged. How wrong I was—again. I don't know why, but I listened to the good doctor, and today, I see the wisdom in his advice.

Finally, in late 1987, I got to a place where I understood that I was powerless and I was beaten. I could not find a way to solve my problems on my own. It was pointed out to me that my best thinking—the absolute most brilliant thoughts I had ever had—finally put me in this place. I had to surrender my old way of thinking completely.

Here is the greatest single realization I've had: Once I accept that I am powerless, I begin to receive power—the power to recover from a seemingly hopeless state of mind and body. It is the ultimate paradox. We surrender to win.

Chapter Eleven
I Believe—Step Two

I believe. I come to believe that a power greater than myself, the Master Mind, can change my life.

LET ME START OFF BY SAYING that I had a very serious problem with organized religion and God in my adolescence and early adult years. I've never been able to connect to the concept of a loving higher power as a father figure. I wish I could today. To me, my father meant potential death. Subsequently, I couldn't hear the message. I couldn't respect authority figures, and if there was one thing the Catholic Church I was raised in was, it was authoritarian.

I have grave doubts about the existence of God. One of the great things about education is that it enables one to learn how to think critically, and not accept precepts just on faith. To enter into dialectic discourse—to question, to ponder and wonder where I fit in the great scheme of things, is one of the great intellectual rewards of a higher education. It's also one of its greatest pitfalls.

The further I went with my education, the less I believed in anything anymore. I had to be able to prove it empirically. At one time, I'd been involved in the Charismatic Renewal for the Catholic Church. I really liked those people. I believe they were genuine and open, but somewhat naïve in their point of view. I must confess that I've always had a problem with fundamentalists. I believe they are good, honest people, but their insistence that the Bible must be believed word for word is a very inflexible position.

It doesn't allow for the cultural times that these stories were written in, or for the fact that the Bible is filled with metaphors and allegories. These were acceptable ways to tell a story so the audience could understand the point being made. Jesus often taught with parables. To think one can sit around drinking poison or getting bit by poisonous snakes, however, is just foolish. It does nothing to further the message that God loves all of us, and He wants us all to love Him and one another as ourselves. This was one of the reasons I became interested in The Pagan Christ.

If that's how their God operates, well, I sure don't want to know or give Him more than a passing thought. It was those kinds of people, however, that created in me my disdain for organized religion. They still do today. But I try and keep an open mind, regardless. There are men like Zander Dunn, a Presbyterian minister on Amherst Island where I used to live, who carries God's message of love and forgiveness and is a real testament to Christ's love. The same for the local Catholic priest, Father Grainger, who was there at the time. He was a very kind and insightful minister. The same is true for Andrew Chisholm at the Anglican Church. I recently attended a Jewish funeral, and that service struck me as being remarkably compassionate.

I'm quite aware of black or white thinking: all or nothing. It is unhealthy psychologically. At its root is perfectionism and pride. No one can live up to the person who has perfectionist ideals or standards. It is a form of codependency that has people operate out of shame and blame. The good news to me today is that I have come to believe that a power greater than myself—a Higher Mind—can change my life. When I choose to sit with one other person, the Bible says, "When two or more are gathered, then I am there too." I paraphrase for the benefit of any pedantic people who insist on exact quotes. I don't think it matters to God what you call him. As long as you know it is God you are speaking to.

I feel fortunate to have visited the Middle East and made friends in Israel. I've had Israeli business partners. There's one Israeli friend in particular I have, who will go nameless, who has many good qualities. He's good, kind, generous, and considerate man. If Jesus were like my friend, I'd like him a lot. That was comforting to me as a North American, because when I think of the historical context of Christ, how they lived, the world they functioned in, it is often difficult for me to personalize Christ. To have an Israeli point of reference was helpful.

Having been raised Roman Catholic, I don't find it hard to pray to Jesus. Do I think he was a divine entity? At times and in an odd way, yes. But I am not certain if He was the only son God ever had. I believe that God has sent other messengers—like Mohamed, like Abraham, and like Buddha. I know to some people that is heterodoxy. For me, however, it is not because it's only a thought I have. If I am wrong, I'm sure God will be big enough to forgive me for being human. After all, He made me imperfect.

When I was in Jerusalem, I was standing in the square that looks over the Dome of the Rock, the

Wailing Wall and the Church of the Holy Sepulcher. As I was standing there, I had a revelation. My personal epiphany was that the founding of three of the world's predominate religions was within a five-iron of each other.

In case you're not a golfer, that is a very short distance.

In communication theory, there is the concept of Punctuation of Sequence of Events. If you take three people, all standing on different corners, and ask them to describe the same event that just transpired—whether it is a car accident or a debate—you will be given three distinct and unrelated answers. If you didn't know they'd been standing at the same corner or present at the same accident, you would never have guessed it. So, here we had a variety of very spiritual individuals, two of them ironically are first cousins, who all heard the same message and interpreted it differently.

We all agree there is one God who is great, but we all choose to call Him by our own ethnocentric names. In fact, for us Westerners, Jesus' name was changed from *Eashoa* probably around 400 or 500 AD to make him more acceptable to Western culture

I am not a theologian, but what I do know is this: I love the concept of the Holy Spirit. It is said that when Jesus left, he promised us that he would send the Holy Spirit, who would be there for us if we called on Him. I'm somewhat embarrassed to admit it, but only recently have I started to utilize the power of the Holy Spirit again. I can talk to God through Him. It gives me a sense of peace, of calmness and of purpose. Yet, I still don't know about the true divinity of Jesus. I don't think any of us do. What separates Christianity for me from all other religions is the resurrection. But when I look at the resurrection stories, I see a lot of them.

So far, it is the only one that has defied death. Yet theories abound. He didn't die; he was unconscious. He was drugged. However, if we are to believe the apostles, if we are to believe their witness, then He did die and rise again. These people were so clearly moved by His post-resurrection appearances that they gladly, fearlessly went out and faced death. As Elaine Pagels said to me, "It takes a lot more faith to believe he didn't exist in the face of some of the evidence." That's what is incredible to me. The ultimate answer will only come for some of us after death.

But what's more significant to me is even if He didn't actually rise again in body, when I choose to believe in some form of higher power—whether it is Jesus, the Holy Spirit, God the Father, nature, or a group of people who have more conscious contact with God than —my life works better. I don't have to subscribe to any religious beliefs to obtain the benefits of spirituality. I just have to believe in a power greater than myself, that can and will help me if I ask for help. My journey back to any belief in God has been extremely slow, and it is not what the traditional mainstream Christian faiths teach per se. But I'm comfortable with it, and to me, that's all that matters. It's the spirit of the teachings, not the law I'm interested in.

If I meet one hundred people who live their lives by self-determination, with no conscious contact or desire for any spiritual connection at all, generally, but not always, they have fairly shallow lives. There are some very committed humanists that I've met over the years, and particularly while I was making the television series *Life After Death*, based on Tom Harpur's book of the same title. Tom is a Rhodes scholar and a very thoughtful man. He is a trained theologian and a graduate of Oxford University.

I investigated various subjects: Is there life after death? Are there angels? Does some part of our consciousness survive after death? What about hell? Does it exist? What about reincarnation? Do we come back?

I have to say at the end of two years of further research and writing based on Tom's research—having spent months in the field talking to people who underwent Near Death Experiences, who had seen manifestations of deceased loved ones as well as scientists, doctors and skeptics—that the evidence was overwhelmingly in favor of the fact that something extraordinary does happen at the time of death. There is no doubt in the minds of those people who have had one of these experiences that it was real.

There are mysteries out there that have no easy explanation. From a purely medical point of view, many of the people we met and interviewed and who had these remarkable experiences should not have lived or survived the traumas they did. Time and time again, I met the physicians who confirmed that fact. Yet here they were. These were sane, conservative, rational people in every area of their lives—except for these occurrences, which defied all known scientific explanation.

The researchers and physicists who are working on these questions are just as puzzled as anyone, because they know that something quite remarkable is happening. The challenge that faces the scientists in this field is they can't replicate these studies in the traditional, empirical paradigm they normally operate within. Therein lies the mystery of it all, and that's where faith is needed.

Getting back to my original point, if we take one hundred people—let's say chronic alcoholics—where society has written them off because they are of the hopeless variety, and they come to believe in a power greater than themselves, a tremendous alteration takes place. While not all of them will stay the course, in case after case these people defy the odds, recover and become useful members of society: fathers, mothers, brothers and sisters.

On the other hand, if you take 100 people, likewise inflicted and who utilize willpower, rational recovery, traditional psychiatry or pharmaceutical therapy—and if you can ever get them to be rigorously honest (which is near impossible for an active alcoholic, such as the old joke goes: "When's an alcoholic lying? When his/her lips are moving.")—their recovery rate is abysmal. It's not likely to exceed 5 percent.

But when they have a spiritual foundation, the statistics are that over 50 percent of those who choose to go for help recover, while approximately 25percent relapse, and then come back after a time. In recent years, treatment centers have influenced those statistics, and that's why I qualify mine to state, "Those who choose to go for help," not those forced to go by employers, spouses or the courts.

That is empirical proof to me.

When I didn't believe in God, I lived in constant fear. In spite of tremendous success in my chosen profession—working with people like Phillip Borsos, Barry Healey and Peter O'Brian, and then having Francis Ford Coppola's company Zoetrope Studios present our movie, I never had more than a fleeting experience of happiness. I was driven to want more. I had no peace of mind, and I was riddled with jealousy and resentment. Why couldn't we get what we wanted? I was always having to deal with people that had never done what we had done creatively, but had the power to approve what we were about to try and do.

More importantly, I felt dislocated from the greater elements of society. I felt estranged from ordinary people because I was so consumed with self. That is why I have such a tremendous respect for people like Stephen Spielberg, Brad Pitt and Martin Sheen, who can remove themselves from the snare of egomaniacal behavior and attempt to help others. They seem like genuinely good men. Ditto for the likes of Susan Sarandon, who often places societal issues ahead of self-aggrandizement.

Bob Rosenblat's friend, Paul Henderson, a club owner and LA entrepreneur, introduced us to numerous renowned people in the entertainment business in Los Angeles. First was Shari Lansing, who turned out to be a very interesting woman. She was president of 20the Century Fox at the time. What struck me about her was that she always took the time to return a call, or when you were in a meeting with her, she was present for you. She made you feel like you were an important person, and she had a remarkable clarity in dealing with people. My experience of her was she had an absolute respect for people. It is why her career has continued to blossom, I'm sure.

Sitting in Robert Evan's home in Beverly Hills, surrounded by more opulence and Hollywood history than I could have ever imagined, was a fascinating experience. Here was the man who produced some of the greatest movies of the all time: *The Godfather* series of films with Francis Coppola, *Chinatown* and *Love Story*. When you walked into his living room, it was like walking into a palace. While nice homes were not new to me, his home in Beverly Hills was beyond anything I'd ever seen. He had a living room that was impeccably furnished. Off his living room and next to the swimming pool was a private screening room. On my second visit there, I was invited to a screening of a new feature that Paramount was going to release. Here was the real Hollywood. I knew that

Jack Nicholson had sat in his living room, along with Bobby Kennedy and every major star of the 60s, 70s and 80s. John Houston, my hero, had also been a guest at his home. These were heady experiences, and ones I'll never forget. He was kind enough to autograph a book he'd written. Yet, I was to find out he was confronting his own demons at this time too. It taught me that you never know what is going on inside someone's life from the outside view, which can often look so appealing. For the vast majority of us who get a chance to operate in that arena (Hollywood)—and believe me, I only got through the gate for a brief glance—it is an emotional minefield, in which very few people survive intact.

I love Hollywood, or the image of Hollywood. It gave me a chance to see that one could acquire tremendous success, and it still didn't guarantee happiness. What is ironic to me is that I was never very happy during the whole process of doing theatrical feature films. There were moments of elation, but no sense of accomplishment. I wish I could have changed the way I felt. But, it was not to be.

When I finally hit bottom after the debacle of *Dixie Lanes* and realized we were in big trouble, I didn't know what to do. When I was back in New York City, as I wrote earlier, I felt overwrought. I really began to question if I could ever change. Would my life ever stop being in chaos and shambles? I wondered to myself.

I was supposed to be enjoying the benefits of our films and the critical success of our previous productions. Instead, I was frantically, desperately trying to get another movie made. I was like a junkie who needed another filmic fix. I knew if I could get one more, my life would be different. Just like all the other times I believed: once I get a new girlfriend, the right car, the right address, the right deal, the right haircut, the right clothes, the right friends, the right city, the degree or degrees, the right amount of money—well, then, you'll see, everything will be just great, fabulous. But it never comes.

There's never enough when all we seek is material wealth, possessions or the acknowledgment and praise of the world. There is no lasting benefit to it. Even though these statements have been pointed out in every inspirational book written in the last several thousand years, I feel as if I just found out, and *wow*! What a great realization it is to come to in my right mind!

But what does last is a belief in a power greater than we are, and a desire to be of service. It gives one purpose. It allows us to experience the pain of change sufficiently, so we can break free of the bondage of self. We can finally let go of the need to prove ourselves to others. We're okay just the way we are. We don't have to become a hotshot producer, writer, doctor, lawyer, poet, candlestick maker, public servant, president of a major corporation, famous politician, or any other 'thing or occupation' that we think is going to change us or our lives.

When we change at our core and become loving, patient and generous human beings, capable of forgiving the worst enemy or the best friend, when we can let go of anger and resentment, incredible events come to pass. All we have to do is keep showing up and asking God for help. Then if we still want it, chances are we can get back into the game of life, realizing that when we undertake projects to be of service—to entertain, to educate or enlighten—then we're on the right path and can expect the right results. We can have all the success we want, and actually enjoy it.

Life ebbs and flows, and I've noticed as the Byrds' song once said back in the 60s, there is time for planting and a time for harvesting, a time for living and a time for dying. We don't necessarily always have to physically die. We can suffer emotional death through depression, rejection or the loss of a loved one. But rebirth—the concept of resurrection—is a wonderful one to live our lives by. We do rise up again. We do come back, if we just don't quit one day too soon.

No matter how bad life is today, if we put the effort in to change, I can promise you that it will be that good tomorrow. In other words, the degree that you are hurting today will be the degree of happiness that you will gain by surrendering and believing in the God of your understanding.

Do we ever stop making mistakes or being weak-willed? Not that I can see. The only things I've done perfectly for the past 25 years is not picking up a drink or a drug. But I've just about done everything else wrong that a human being can. Each mistake I've made has contributed to my growth. Embrace change. Make mistakes. They all lead to the right answer eventually. Worrying about making mistakes keeps us locked into unhealthy perfectionist thinking, and expectations about others and ourselves.

Coming to believe in a Power greater than you is the best formula I know of to change our lives. If you could have your own concept of God, what or who would it be?

I had a major realization sitting in a little Catholic church a few years ago. I was glancing out the window—recently decorated for Thanksgiving and the beginning of Advent (heading into Christmas)—when I saw the light refract through a crystal that had been hung in the window. The day was sunny and bright. The light shone through the prism, reflecting the colors blue, green and yellow. I was watching them bounce off the walls, and suddenly they landed on the Chalice. At once, I had the realization that I had worshipped false idols. They took the form of Academy Awards.

My whole life had been devoted to trying to get one. Our Canadian Awards are also Golden Statues. Though our productions did win many awards, I never acquired the sense that I'd accomplished anything. Then it really hit me. I understood that I'd been chasing the wrong gods all my life.

I'm not deprecating material achievement. Given the choice, I'd rather live any day in comfort, surrounded by beauty and nice possessions. I enjoy a nice home, which I have today. I enjoy driving nice cars. One day I hope to get an old '67 Corvette. I've always wanted one. Or I would like a '57 Chevy convertible. I would dearly love a 28-foot sailboat. I believe today it is okay for me to have one. But if I don't get it, it won't be the end of the world. My friend Richard has one, and he invites me out frequently with my kids.

This is one of the toughest areas in my life that I have to work the hardest on. *I am a worthy human being. I deserve a nice home, good transportation. I deserve a good income. I deserve a happy and peaceful family life. I deserve to be debt free.* These are affirmations I must continue to feed into my mind, like you would a new software program into a computer, to counteract all of the negative messages I received in my childhood.

Here's the crux of the problem for me. When I keep chasing money or a career at the cost of my personal life and my relations, it is counterproductive. When I am never home because I am a workaholic, it is hard on my children and my relationships. Furthermore, when my focus is on obtaining material possessions to make myself feel good, or to be acceptable to society or my peers, the experience is empty, hollow and leads to just wanting more. I can never fill the emotional hole I feel inside myself with material possessions. No matter how much I buy, it is never going to be enough. This is another one of the lies my mind tells me. I don't have the right possessions, but if I go to the right store, then this time, I'll be happy. I won't, you won't, and it will never happen.

Balance is the key. When I believe in a Power greater than myself, when I believe that this Power can change the way I think, feel and act, I am finally on the road to liberation. I will begin to know a joy and a happiness that I never experienced. I will be able to forgive myself for being human and making mistakes. I will not be plagued by perfectionism. I will become more patient and loving, or at least more so than I ever was. If you want to find out how you're doing in life, ask your immediate family or your romantic partner. Do they share the same vision of your life as you do? Good question. Be grateful for what you already have. Give thanks frequently for the things that matter in your life, like your health and the health of your family. Write a list in the front of a notebook or your day timer, and look at it every day.

It is good to ask God to guide us in all our affairs. If we come to believe, then I can turn over my relationship with Kathy, who is my life today and who I am so grateful for. I am given peace when I would normally blow up and overreact. If I do blow up, which I do occasionally now, I am able to admit I was wrong and apologize to my sweetheart, co-workers or kids. I am able to be more patient with my children. When I believe in God, I am able to let go of results in my life: writing exams, getting a job, acquiring a raise or promotion, or writing this book or waiting for networks or studios to get back to me on projects. I can ask to be guided in my choice of career. I can ask God to help me in my family relations. Feuds of long standing can melt away miraculously and mysteriously when I release the results to the God of my understanding. I will find that I am filled with a new sense of optimism about the future, regardless of what the previous circumstances were.

You may have deep-seated emotional and mental problems. They can be helped too. All it takes is a willingness to believe.

The question I have is, what do you have to lose by trying it for ninety days? Find a group of like-minded people. They are everywhere. Churches, social gatherings, clubs. They are people just like you and me looking for answers. The common bond that holds all of us together is that we believe in a Power greater than we are: God as you understand him or her to be. As a result of our beliefs, our lives have been changed at every level: spiritually, emotionally, physically and financially.

Chapter Twelve
I Am Ready To Be Changed—Step Three

I realize that erroneous self-defeating thinking is the cause of my problems, unhappiness, fears and failures.

I HAVE BEEN PLAGUED my whole life with self-doubt, low self-esteem, and a fear of failure. People who don't know me are often shocked when I say these things. "How can that be when you've done so well?" is the most common question I'm asked.

These feelings and emotions have immobilized me at times, and at others, caused me to overreact in very unhealthy ways. When filled with fear, I become too aggressive. In compensating for these feelings, I become arrogant, while filled with insecurity. Many people in Hollywood operate out of this psychological model. I refer to it as "egocentric megalomaniacs with low self-esteem."

It is best summed up in an old Zen saying, "An empty vessel makes the loudest noise." It is imperative for me to realize that my self-defeating thinking is the cause of my problems, unhappiness, fears and failures.

What are the traits that keep me locked into this behavior? First: thinking of myself as a victim. I was victimized as a child, and unconsciously I've carried that into my adult life. It is neither healthy nor constructive, and it can be changed. I have often blamed others for the way I feel, and I've never stood up for myself when I have been wronged. I've been afraid to tell people what I really think for fear of rejection. I didn't want anyone else rejecting me...after my father had.

But giving away one's power—that is, not taking care of myself appropriately—leads to depression, anger and resentment. If I don't know how to take care of myself, how can I ever hope to properly enter into an equal partnership with another human being, whether it's my wife, life partner, a business partner or a true friend? If I don't change, I will lack integrity and courage, because I'm always at the whim of what others think of me. I'm afraid to take a stand, or I only take stands in order to dominate and be popular. Once again, extremes seem to play an integral part in this way of being.

Being a victim also creates the potential for rage—misappropriate rage at the wrong people, at the wrong time, in the wrong places. How do we cope with these feelings? We begin to utilize inappropriate activities to change the way we feel. We seek highs in work, alcohol, drugs, food, or sex, to name just a few. We become chronic overachievers who are constantly left with depression, because once the high of the accomplishment is gone, we are left with these uneasy feelings of inadequacy. This paradigm leads to 'all or nothing' thinking.

We often seek out individuals or situations that are not healthy for us, or unavailable to us. When we achieve what we want from them, then we withdraw, hurting them and others. When we are attracted to relationships or seek out persons who are not available to us, it is a form of juvenile selfishness and self-centeredness.

When we don't get what we want, we withdraw and become reclusive. We isolate, feeling sorry for ourselves. We plot revenge, or we gossip with the intention of destroying reputations and careers by spreading untruths. This can only lead to depression and will always come back on you or me—in exactly the same form as we put it out. It may take years, but I guarantee, it will happen. What is at the root of this dilemma? Number one is pride, followed closely by fear, resentment and envy.

What happens is: I become afraid of being less than perfect. I won't allow myself to go to social or work events and enjoy the company of my wife or romantic partner, for fear of not being liked by her friends or fear that I may be judged by others because I don't have the right job, or I don't wear the right clothes. I may not have traveled in the right social circles growing up. Or, like me, you may have been someone that grew up in a good neighborhood, but you were the only child whose parents had separated, or your mother had to work like mine did, while all the other kids' parents had professional or executive occupations. These kinds of feelings, these insecurities from our childhoods, stay with us and haunt us in our mature years.

I may feel insecure about my economic future because my colleagues at work may judge me harshly. As a result of my inability to socialize, my job may be at risk—especially if I have an occupation that demands I interact socially. In truth, what's being threatened is our self-esteem and our financial future. That really crippled me when I was a young producer.

I would sit in the middle of crowds at film festivals, and even though our work had already been judged to be very good, I would be riddled with insecurity. I can remember sitting at the Banff

Television Festival several years ago, where I was appearing on a panel. There was a large crowd, numbering in the hundreds of people, waiting to hear us speak. I was filled with dread and a sense that I didn't belong there. I hadn't done enough. I didn't deserve to be on the podium. Then, as my mind calmed down and I glanced around, I noticed that there might have been a half-dozen people in the room that had done as much or more than me. I had written, produced, executive produced or acted as a creative consultant on over 100 television episodes. In addition, I had major feature film credits, and yet somehow, I imagined that all these people were better than I was. Now, I didn't go off on an ego trip about it. I just recognized how my mind lies to me. I was as talented as most of the people in that room. My track record spoke for itself.

I am also arrogant at times. I feel superior to others, until I meet someone more successful than I am, and then I revert to insecurity. I sometimes try to be the center of attention. I speak and act so I will be noticed. I try and impress others, because it makes me feel better to think I'm someone special, and I want you to know, too. I'm grateful to say that most of those traits have really decreased significantly over the years, but they did plague me when I was younger. It's very embarrassing now to think back on what an obnoxious young man I was at times.

Here are the symptoms of codependency according to Adult Children of Alcoholics and Dysfunctional Families: My good feelings about who I am stem from being liked by you. My good feelings about who I am stem from receiving approval from you. Your struggles affect my serenity. My mental attention focuses on solving your problems, on relieving your pain. My attention is focused on pleasing you. My attention is focused on protecting you. My attention is focused on manipulating you to 'do it my way.' Relieving your pain bolsters my self-esteem. My own hobbies and interests are put aside in favor of sharing your interests and hobbies.

Because I feel you are a reflection of me, I want your behavior and personal appearance to be dictated by my desires. I am aware of what you feel and want, rather than of what I feel and want. Even when I am not truly aware, I assume that I am. The dreams I have for my future are linked to you. My fear of rejection determines what I say and do. My fear of anger determines what I say and do. I use giving as a way of feeling safe in our relationship. My social circle diminishes as I involve myself with you. I put my values aside in order to connect with you. I value your opinion and way of doing things more than my own. The quality of life varies in relation to the quality of yours.

It's never quite as simple as it sounds. Anger is the outward manifestation of my old thinking. Many times in life, we suppress anger. That can turn into depression. Or we take it out on the wrong people, or on an unsuspecting person who happens to be the hapless victim of our unexpressed rage.

I believe the cause of these feelings for me was coming out of such a chaotic home. I had to have order. It represented manageability to me. The feelings that get triggered in me are resentment, self-pity, jealousy, prejudice, depression and physical illness.

When I get angry, I pout. I become aggressive and yell. I get agitated when I'm driving. I find myself suffering from road rage. At home or at work, I withdraw and I begin to act like a kid. Why? Because that's the learned model I'm operating from. When these feelings surface, they make no sense at all to an adult. That's because my frightened six-year-old emotional self has wrestled control of my emotions from my adult, rational, conscious mind.

Chronic infantile omnipotence has taken over. Metaphorically, I lie on the floor, kicking and screaming until I get my own way. Works when you're six. Not at thirty-six, forty-six or, God forbid, fifty-six. Of course our unconscious is not stupid. It finds wonderful ways to mask the process so I don't look quite so immature. I cover it in a blanket of rationalization. It's your fault. Not mine. And I'm only too glad to help you by pointing out your deficiencies, so you can grow as a person. Bovine Scatology. I'm just rationalizing my point of view.

At the root of these feelings are insecurity, anxiety and resentment. What is at risk is my self-esteem, my goals, or my personal or sexual relations.

What is important for me to do is to learn how to appropriately express my anger. When I feel like kicking the dog, slamming a door or yelling at one of the kids or my partner, I have to cool down, calm down and simply say, "I feel angry and upset." Nobody can argue with my feelings. It's not up for discussion. But they also have the right to defend their actions, and I had better be prepared to hear what they have to say. I may not like it one bit. Nevertheless, their feelings are as legitimate as mine.

What generally triggers me is the fear that I won't get what I want, or I will lose something I already have. That pushes me over the edge. If we're reducing our spending, I can't drive a new German sports car. Now I have a nice car from the US. Much more economical, less pollution, but my ego does handstands because I don't have my toys anymore.

I say to my mind, "Thanks for sharing. Now get lost." The fact is, my new vehicle is a great car, has a nice sunroof, a great sound system, and consumes about fifty percent less gas. I'm helping the environment, and helping my bottom line because it costs me half as much to operate. I am not what I drive, in spite of the propaganda to get me to believe I am. It doesn't mean I might not go out and get another luxury automobile one day. I just know today, it is a one-way love affair. For me, the thrill of new cars lasts about two to three months, and then I think, why am I spending all this money? I'm no sooner off the lot than my mind says, "Why didn't you get the Hemi? Why didn't you get the other model, the convertible? That's the one that would have really made you happy."

I can't emphasize this enough. I really have to treat my ego as if it's a third person. Otherwise, it just runs the living hell out of me, and is soon joined by a whole board of directors in my head that loves to add their two cents. Especially around 4 a.m.

We won't have enough money, so I want to hoard it. Instead of realizing that I have talents and abilities, I can earn a reasonable living, but I still go into a panic. I think I'll never make another dime again. This is old, unhealthy thinking that can only be replaced when I let go absolutely and trust that I will be guided in all departments of my life.

Further means of trying to control include overreacting to change. As a child, I had little control over the behavior of my father, or the things that happened in our home. As I grew older, I tried to control the feelings and behavior of others. This exemplifies itself in interpersonal relations when I have to do everything myself, because no one will do it as well as I will. That only leads to passive-aggressive behavior from others who become fed up with trying to be controlled. They resent it. Or they have such a sick need to be 'saved, fixed, taken care of" that we generally end up getting rid of them because they drive us crazy with all of their needs. We are like magnets that attract needy people. Or, like a magnet which has a polar opposite, we repel people with our unhealthy behavior.

We also demonstrate rigid behavior. There is no room for spontaneity—we become extremely upset when any of our plans are interrupted. We worry about being late. We become inflexible in our dealings with others in planning social or work events. This in turn creates stress and anxiety in our friends, partners and work associates. Compromise is a deadly disease to this way of thinking.

I would go to great lengths to manage how others saw me. I had a fear of "looking bad." The main mantra of my mother when I was a child was, "What will the neighbors think?"

Well, quite frankly, I don't give a damn anymore. I had a chance to talk to my mother before she died. When she was eighty years old, I invited her to take a workshop with me. It was based on a workbook *The Twelve Steps: A Way Out* for Adult Children of Alcoholics and Dysfunctional Families. It was very valuable. I was able to share with her how much her fear-based behavior had scarred me, because I was terrified down to my core of what others thought of me. I did it in a very gentle way. She got it, and we were able to resolve that this was just part of the process for both of us to let go of our old beliefs.

Twenty-six weeks to the day after she completed the workshop, she stood up for the first time and thanked everyone in the room. She asked me to come over to her house later that week. At first she was as calm as could be, and then she just started crying. She admitted to me for the first time in my life that she'd carried around so much shame because she'd never been able to go to university—she wanted to be a doctor when she was a young girl in the 1920s. Her father didn't believe women should be educated. She had to run away from home and move in with the Grey Nuns in Timmins, so she could go into nursing school. She never finished high school and felt incredible shame because of it.

She was also angry because on many occasions she had to step in and fix mistakes young doctors had made, without ever being acknowledged for her contribution. I had no idea that she felt this way. Here I was in my mid-forties, and I'd never had a conversation with my mother anywhere close to this level. I couldn't believe how devastated she was.

She felt that it was her fault I'd ended up an alcoholic like my father. I pointed out to her that, in my judgment, I'd inherited a condition no different than diabetes. It wasn't her fault. It had more to do with genetics, which I'm convinced beyond any shadow of a doubt was the primary cause. There was no doubt I was influenced by our alcoholic home, but the fact is, once I ingested alcohol, I felt different. It was a chemical reaction. I had a physical allergy. She or my father didn't hold me down in high school when I was feeling so insecure and say, "Here, take a big slug of this, and you'll feel better." Quite the opposite! She tried in myriad ways to help me.

She then went on to tell me that she'd always wanted to be a writer, too. She'd written a story that she wanted me to read. I still have it today. Then she said, "What do you want here in the house?"

I looked around our old family home and asked her, "Why are you asking me this now?"

"I just want to get my affairs in order," she replied. "Now I can die in peace."

For the first time in almost forty years, she was free of the guilt that somehow she'd made major mistakes with my father, my brothers and sisters, and me. She was able to let go of blaming herself for our childhoods. She had contacted my two sisters and made amends to both of them. I believe both my sisters appreciated that tremendously. It was miraculous to see. I told her to just relax. I was just grateful to see that she was so happy.

Eight weeks later, she lapsed into a coma at Woman's College Hospital after she made me promise that I would take care of her West Highland terrier, Shorty. Eight weeks before her bout, she was in fair health, but she was ready to die and really just too tired of life to go on any further.

Years of cancer treatments and her congestive heart failure all took their toll on her, but now she felt secure enough about our futures to finally let go. I remember the morning after she'd asked me to take care of her little dog, Shorty, when I showed up at the hospital and there was a woman lying there who wasn't my mother. She'd had a stroke in the night. I spoke to the doctor, and he confirmed to me that she was in the process of dying. I just let go and felt the loss in a very healthy, emotional way.

My mother wouldn't die with all us in her hospital room. She waited for us to go home. Finally, with just my oldest brother Robert there, she came to, looked at him and passed on.

Being there for her those last few days of her life was the most rewarding experience of my adult life. I am so grateful that I was there, not having to control the outcome of her death. I could let go absolutely. *Let go and let God.*

What my mother demonstrated to me was trust. The very thing I couldn't do with my father, I could do with my mother. She never let me down once. If something was promised, she delivered. In retrospect, I am astounded that she was able to do so much for me. I was a kid with a lot of demands growing up. How she ever met half of her undertakings is a miracle to me. Now, with children of my own, I see how difficult it must have been for her, with no support whatsoever from my father.

But trust still remains a key issue for me today. It doesn't come easily to me. I still worry about how things will turn out. I find it hard to believe that people have my best interests at heart. Given the nature of our home growing up, why am I so surprised? But worry is a true waste of time. Study after study has demonstrated that 95 percent of what people worry about never comes to pass. It's just the chattering of our mind—the incessant need to keep rolling. Think of the rotisserie I mentioned earlier that just keeps spinning around; first, it's money, then my looks, my health, death, then my career, taxes—it just keeps spinning, going nowhere. That's another area where I've learned to just thank my mind for sharing.

Another element of unhealthy thinking is intolerance. I become judgmental, overly critical of my wife, my kids, my associates in business, and the guy who drives the bus, the waitress in the restaurant. If I am not in a healthy state of mind, my thinking takes on a strange twist.

I become intolerant of others who don't share my ethno-specific background or looks. If you're Arab on a flight with me, do I look at you with suspicion after September 11, 2001? Yes! If I said "No," I'd be a liar. So how do I overcome that intolerance? By making sure I go out of my way to get to know someone who is a Muslim, or an Arab. In my case it was meeting a Palestinian family a few years ago, when I was doing the series *Counter*

Force. When we went into the Gaza Strip, we were invited into the home of a local Palestinian family. They probably spent a week's wages to ensure that we had the most delicious coffee and sweets I'd ever eaten.

Yet they had a child who was critically ill, lying in the living room. They had no money to pay for a doctor. When we offered to give them money for his treatment, they were offended. They had their pride. They were self-supporting and didn't want charity. Inside I felt sick, and I went to Mustafa, our Palestinian driver, and asked him what to do. He instructed me to put some money under the child's mattress as a present to him—to wink, but not say anything. We left the US currency, winked, and I patted the boy on the head and thanked our hosts for a truly enlightening evening. After that visit, word got around the local camps in Gaza so quickly that we were invited to go out for a walk through the streets that are seen night after night on North American and European television during the uprising, where young Palestinians throw rocks at Israeli soldiers. At no time did I feel fear. I'm grateful to say that there are just as many Israelis who are also trying desperately to find a solution to the whole mess.

A few years ago, when I was married to Deb, we were invited with three other couples to a Winter Solstice party put on by one of my former sisters-in-law. She's a physician and psychotherapist, and is very interested in things spiritual. Her husband, Don, is a professor. He invited another electrical engineer, Mohammad, and his wife. They were both Muslims from North Africa. It was enlightening and enjoyable. Once again, we all learned a great deal more when we entered that home for dinner. Each one of us contributed to the understanding of our culture and our belief system, so that each of us was given a gift of knowledge. It contributed to a very pleasant Christmas and recognition of the origin of many of our Judaic/Christian/Muslim traditions.

When I look back at my upbringing, my father was probably anti-Semitic. As a result, I went out of my way to meet other kids who were Jewish when I was growing up. Why was my father so bigoted, I wondered? As I also mentioned earlier, you weren't much better if you were Protestant, either. I'm sure those families who were members of the Orange Lodge would have the same feelings about us Catholics.

I ended up with several Jewish and Israeli business partners, and discovered I had a lot in common with them in coming from an Irish background. Both were matriarchal societies in spite of the fact that the males, on the surface, tended to dominate socially. We both are riddled with guilt and neuroses. Well, the Jews have neuroses, and we have guilt—Irish-Catholic guilt. It's all the same.

We were both very oppressed races at one time. In Ireland, over one million men, women and children died at the side of the roads where the famine walls were built, while food rotted in Cork and Dublin. The British believed the people would become dependent on them if they fed them during the potato famine. Millions of others were driven from their land and forced to emigrate to North America and Australia. Given that the population of Ireland has never really exceeded much over four million, it was a tremendous loss. It is a time in my ancestral history that gives me real empathy for the suffering of those six million plus, who either lost their lives or were displaced in the Holocaust.

Both races were looked down upon at the turn of the century, in North America and throughout the world. You had your Irish ghetto and your Jewish ghetto and your black ghettos. There are a lot of striking similarities. Both races are incredibly spiritual and religious. Both are God-centered. Both races have contributed significantly to modern culture, but many are unaware of the Irish contributions in literature, great story-telling, and a prolific culture that saved the great texts from the Dark Ages and, last but not least, great beer and whiskey—the Irish curse. There's a wonderful book entitled *How the Irish Saved Civilization: The Untold Story of Ireland's Heroic Role from the Fall of Rome to the Rise of Medieval Europe* by Thomas Cahill. I can't recommend this book highly enough. He also wrote a companion piece titled *The Gifts of the Jews,* which is also well worth reading.

Now I'm not interested in hearing from any historians, anthropologists or sociologists about a few misstated facts that I may not have presented quite accurately. I know a lot of people will insist that Judaism is a patriarchal society, but I challenge anyone to go into the home and tell that to a Jewish mother. Won't happen. It is another Irish tendency not to let a mistake get in the way of a great story. My point in stating the previous information is that I had to go out and break the family mold, so I wouldn't be intolerant.

The irony is my father and his father lost money when their company's stock was shorted by a well-known Jewish financier in New York, sometime back in the 40s. My dad never forgave him for that. Yet it was my Jewish backers who saved me on more than one occasion. Interesting how that works out.

Fear of abandonment is another old way of thinking. It wasn't until I was in my forties that I was able to come to grip with this element of my life. I found it difficult to get close to people. I was a loner. I didn't like exposing my work or my ideas to others, for fear of criticism. Where does it stem from? Well, in my case, not knowing what to think because of the insanity of my upbringing. First, I had absolutely no emotional or intellectual encouragement. I was never told I had any ability, or that I was ever good at anything. I had no support for any of my talents. I had to learn how to self-actualize at a very young age.

Those feelings were amplified because I never knew who was going to come through the door when I was a child. It was awful waiting to see what kind of shape my father was going to be in. Then, when my mother moved us to Toronto, I just felt this incredible loss of identity and connection to home. I realize today that I was totally numb. I missed my father a great deal in those first two years. I was grateful that my mother let me call him occasionally. Invariably, he had nothing to say to me. He would inevitably be drunk when I called him, and I realized he'd totally abandoned me as his child.

When I was young, I tried everything at first to please him. I would offer to go get him his slippers. I wanted peace in our house. I would plead with him not to scream at us, not to get his belt and beat my brothers with it, not to get the gun out again. As his alcoholism progressed, my interventions became more and more meaningless to him. His initial abandonment was emotional; then it was followed by his physical departure from our lives. Given the choice, my father chose to move into the Empire Hotel in Timmins, so he could drink himself to death, undisturbed, instead of seeking help to overcome his alcoholism and retain his family. That was the ultimate abandonment. Yet, when I stood at the same crossroads years later, I was able to make the opposite choice. That to me is a miracle, because I know how badly I wanted to go on using.

In later years, this trait manifested itself in me picking people that would abandon me in relationships. First, it was in business, and then in my emotional and romantic life. In romantic relationships, I was filled with insecurity. I would start off by being a caretaker, trying to fix things—if you felt bad, it was my fault. I couldn't just let you have a bad day. I would have to fix it.

How I felt about myself was tied directly to what others thought of me. I was constantly trying to defuse disputes. I hated confrontations. I would go to incredible lengths to manipulate people and situations to get what I wanted. Then, when they either got what they wanted or the price of my neediness was too high, they would head for the hills. Ironically, I would explode under the most bizarre circumstances, often fueled by cocaine or my emotions. Then others would stand in a state of shock as the rage poured out of me, onto mainly unsuspecting poor unfortunates who happened to have met up with me on the day when I was feeling particularly vulnerable.

This is why I desperately wanted money. I thought, if I am rich, then I don't need anyone. I will be all right on my own. It also caused me to be standoffish with people. They thought I was arrogant. I wasn't. I was afraid. It's why, when I walked into a roomful of strangers, I was terrified, and I would position myself off in a corner. My second choice was to go get loaded, so I could walk over to a young lady and be funny. It's why high school and university were so difficult. I actually yearned to get close to people, but the very walls I'd constructed as a child to survive, that were like a reinforced bunker to stop the pain, now became my prison. I couldn't get out, and no one could get in.

When I stood up for myself, I was filled with shame and guilt. I didn't feel I was worthy. The problem must be mine. I was loyal to a fault, and on several occasions, it came back and kicked me in the ass. I now believe I'm over it—hopefully. It gets really boring after a while. Once again, what's at the root of it? Pride and low self-esteem are the primary culprits.

So, the way I overcome it is to trust in my Higher Power. When I do that, my self-esteem increases. I am then able to let go of my need to keep acting out these unhealthy behaviors. I am able to find people who will be there for me when I need them. That is the single greatest thing I've noticed over these past fifteen years. Today I have people I can totally trust. They are there for me through thick and thin. It is also imperative for me to let go and trust, so I can outgrow my need for abandonment. People do leave for a variety of reasons. I must let go of the fear, or it will keep me locked into this unhealthy behavior. Fear, like resentment, is as fatal as cancer. It will eat away at our lives until we are simply shadows of ourselves. When I confront fear head-on, it dissipates every time. Franklin D. Roosevelt said it best: "We have nothing to fear but fear itself."

Chapter Thirteen
I Decide To Be Changed—Step Four

I make decisions to surrender my will and my life to the Higher Mind; I ask to be changed at depth.

TEN YEARS AGO I had a serious reversal in business. Unlike the old days, I didn't let it foster. I was able to express how I felt about the situation to friends, family and associates. At first I was filled with rage and resentment against the two men I was in business with. I called them up and sent scathing emails. I was aggressive and unkind. I did have legitimate reasons to be upset. But my reactions were totally inappropriate when I walked out of the company and gave my power away. I should have sought legal advice.

So, *where had I been wrong?* I asked myself. Was this the first time I'd ended up on the losing side of a business deal? No! Then why now? Why was I feeling everthing I was feeling? As I began to take a serious look at what had gone wrong and what I'd done—an inventory of my part in it, a pattern began to emerge.

I was overly open in my dealings with one of my associates I believe in retrospect he was so afraid of other men, and in some odd way, for him to admit that he was wrong about our other partner was too much for him and it created an inability for him to go on with the me. But his fear caused him to take actions that in my estimation were a massive overreaction, but his prerogative.

But what was really at the source of how I felt? When I went to my spiritual adviser and sought his help, we began to look at what I was feeling. I felt betrayed. I felt hurt. I felt that my contribution was not acknowledged, and that I was becoming the scapegoat for another person's grave problems.

In a very unhealthy way, the blame had been shifted over to me for another's deceitful actions. This time I was able to remove myself from the situation, although it created serious financial loss and uncertainty in my life. Nevertheless, I kept my integrity. Coincidentally, I've ended up with something I've always dreamt of: a house in the country. Have we gone hungry? No. Do I still feel the anger I did? By and large, it is gone. In fact, today I am feeling more peaceful than I ever have at any time in my life. Occasionally I will think about how the situation ended up and, depending on my mood, I might begin to contemplate the sadness I feel over the circumstances. But generally, I am able to accept the state of affairs as exactly the way they are supposed to be.

When I made the decision to leave the company I'd founded, and to leave Toronto, I was very apprehensive. What would I do to earn a living? How could we survive? Would we actually like living so far away from a major metropolitan center? We were heading to the country—far away from the center of my industry, but Deb and I really wanted to see if we could make a change, a significant change in our lives. I knew that if we didn't do it, then we never would. Our two kids were eleven and twelve, and we knew if we put it off, we wouldn't be able to do it once they hit their teens. It wouldn't have been fair to them. Plus, we decided we would give it two years, and if we hated it we could always move back to the city.

So here was a case of confronting old thinking—unhealthy thinking—and saying, "I'm not going to do what I've always done."

I wasn't going to stay and get into litigation and crazy name-calling, which is what might have happened if I'd stayed in our old neighborhood. I would try something different this time. I made the decision to surrender my will and my life to God, as I understood Him. I made the decision to pursue an idea I'd been talking about for over twenty years. I would see if I could write a book about my experiences growing up, and use that as the basis of a new career as an inspirational writer and speaker.

When I ask to be changed, at depth I am heading into new territory. I must confess that it is frightening and very uncomfortable. I knew that I couldn't stay in the company any more, because it was an emotionally unhealthy situation for me to be in. I can't afford emotionally unhealthy people in my life today. It doesn't mean that my former friend can't find a solution to his own dilemma and we can't be friends again, either. I believe in God's world, all things are possible

But, for today, I need to keep my distance. When I see either one, which I do, I am able to be civil, say hello, wish them the best and mean it, and then move on. Here is one of the most important lessons I've had to learn: I can't afford resentment. The analogy is, I drink poison and sit around and wait for you to die.

Resentment will kill me. You may think I'm being over-dramatic. I'm not. How many heart attacks, how many murders, how many lives have been ruined because of perceived wrongs others have done us, and our inability to forgive, forget and move on? Think of the effects of resentment in the case of the hockey father here in Ontario, who killed another father a few years ago because of his resentment.

When we have faith in God, when we are able to be in a Master Mind Group, when we continue to support ourselves and others in a healthy way, life does work out. It does get better, and we do feel at peace again.

It was extremely difficult making the decision to leave my company and getting to a place of forgiveness and release. I went through a period of whining about it, blaming and shaming before I got to acceptance. Acceptance is the answer to all my problems. It really is. When I try to avoid pain—particularly the pain of change—I stay locked into self-destructive behavior longer than it is necessary. When I can accept that change is needed and simply embrace it, I begin to move through the process of healing and forgiving myself, and others, much faster. I am able to get over the sleepless nights, the constant replaying of the situation in my mind. *I should have, if only I'd...those bastards.* It goes on ad nauseum, and I don't find a solution.

I had to be changed at depth to undergo a personal transformation. If I hadn't made the decision to leave my old company, I wouldn't be sitting here today, writing this book. I wouldn't be glancing out my window at the beautiful Bay of Quinte, or spending the time I am in California with a new relationship that just happened after being separated and divorced. I wouldn't be working out three days a week at the great pool where I do. I wouldn't be filled with the gratitude I have for my life today.

No, instead I would be filled with rage and resentment at having to supplicate my desires because I was afraid to give up a paycheck. I would hate myself for being a coward. I would hate myself because I hadn't had the courage to stick up for what I knew was right. That was a major learning experience for me. When I believe in a higher power, when I trust I will be taken care of, I can move on in my life and change the way I see things. By the way, time has proven me right, too. The partner that had created the difficulties has now been removed from the company and is today in dire straits. It's my sincere hope that he is able to find a solution to all his challenges and problems.

I don't care, to the degree I once did, what people think of me today. I thank both my former partners for being great teachers. I have learned so much about human behavior, and myself, from the experience of letting go and trusting it would all work out. And, if I were to realize I was in the wrong, I could go to them and acknowledge it, too. That to me is one of the greatest gifts I've ever received in my life.

What I find particularly unintentional, is that this situation is identical to ones I created many years ago, only the tables had been totally reversed on me this time. I also got to see that I'd finally cleaned the Karmic slate. I am now free of old thinking and acting. I am free. Free to pursue a new way of life, a new way of thinking—one that allows me to recognize that my old thinking was harmful to my health, both physically and psychologically.

So, when I turn my will and life over to God, and ask to be changed at depth, what does that look like in practical terms? Do I sit around the Bhodi tree waiting for a message? I don't think so. Part of my malady was trying to control. I felt that, if I were not in control, then I was definitely headed toward some catastrophic experience.

I begin by simply making a decision. I decide that doing it my way has not worked. It may have produced certain positive results. I was quite successful at getting projects accomplished. I was successful raising money. I did have some truly amazing parties, which I will be grateful for until the day I die. But I was unsuccessful holding onto anything. Further, the price I paid for my accomplishments—the cost emotionally and physically—was exceptionally high. As I wrote earlier, there was no peace of mind. No sense of accomplishment. There was no sense of community. I never had anyone to share any of my great moments with, except a host of drug-induced, fair-weather friends.

I had to let go of old ideas completely. When I stopped drinking at twenty-two years of age, all I did was stop drinking. I didn't change any parts of my personality. I was unwilling to surrender to the concept of a Higher Power. I was unwilling to give up my character defects. I was totally unwilling to trust that God would guide me. Instead, I only called upon God when I was in serious trouble. I expected Him to become a pitch hitter for me, but, I was to discover, that's not how God operates.

Making the decision to change posed a very serious moral dilemma for me. First, I imagined that I would stop having to be cool. Now let me assure you, cool was more a figment of my imagination than reality. While I was fairly cool in my dress, my attitude and my outlook were as conservative as could be—and I successfully hid it from really cool people. I was a phony cool. I was so traditional, so conservative, that it hurt. Deep down, I shocked myself with my actions.

My second big moral dilemma had to do with my fear that I would end up a religious whacko— especially the kind I did not hold in high regard. I thought, if I really decide to turn my will and life over to the care of God, then I'm going to have to stand on the street corner and sing for my supper as I'm screaming, "The end is nigh."

I don't mean to denigrate the work of those who do this. I just wouldn't have the courage of conviction that they do. I identified more with Monty Python's *Life of Brian* than I did with mainstream religion. I can't tell you how afraid I was that this was going to happen to me.

So, I began taking small steps. I was willing to surrender my anger. That was causing me tremendous difficulties at home. I remember yelling at my young son, Brendan, one morning when he was about three or four, and he started to cower. He was terrified of me. There I was my father again, and this time, I had no alcohol or drugs as an excuse. It shocked me that I could be this way. I had to absolutely surrender this character defect. By the way, that son, who is now 23, has worked with me for the past few years, and I think we've had one harsh word in that period of time. We change! That's the good news.

Making the decision to give up anger was an interesting experience. The more I prayed to have my anger removed, the more often I became angry. I was stuck behind idiots that couldn't drive. I had people giving me the finger in traffic. My ex-wife seemed to be more difficult. The kids were acting up more than ever, and I felt like Sisyphus in the Greek myth who pushes the boulder up to the top of the mountain, only to have it roll right back down again. The more committed I was to having anger removed, the more opportunities and situations involving anger kept coming up.

I asked to have fear removed. The moment I did that, I was confronted by situations that created significant amounts of terror. First was fear of financial insecurity. I have been self-employed my whole life—with the exception of teaching at two universities, which I did for almost ten years. I've always had to fend for myself. I couldn't reconcile how it would be okay for me to turn my business and financial life over to God, but here I was in a constant state of dread about our financial future.

He might be okay at things spiritual, but how about a profit-and-loss statement? How about a business plan? What about sales? Being a producer is this generation's version of being a traveling salesman. I go to one of the Meccas of entertainment—Los Angeles, New York or Cannes. I have my bag of goodies: a script, a commitment from a director, perhaps a star attached, a deal with a Canadian broadcaster and a European one, and I do a little dog-and-pony show for some poor executive that has as much interest in hearing what I have to say as he/she does in getting hemorrhoids, because it's just another pitch.

The only difference between me and the countless others trying to do what I do is I've done it enough times successfully that I create a horrible situation for these executives. They're actually filled with anxiety because I have done it before, and this presents two dilemmas for them. First, I might have a winner, and if they say yes, and it isn't, then they could be fired, or humiliated. Second, if they turn me down, they know I'm going across the street where they might say yes, and then when their meeting log is reviewed by the head of development and they realize they turned down this project, and it was successful, then they might get fired.

Hollywood is the only town in the world where you can die of encouragement. People often don't want or know how to say *no*, so they keep saying *maybe*. They might as well say, "We'll give you a deal when the hunchback of Notre Dame straightens out." But, I have found out God does work occasionally—not too often, mind you—but he does hang out a bit in LA. Those people know who they are.

One of the ongoing fears I've had is about not being able to pay off all of my creditors. Initially I was very frightened to contact them. I had to change this. So beginning about twenty-four years ago, I started to call, write or visit as many as I could find. I was very nervous and self-conscious contacting the ones who'd wanted to sue me for *Dixie Lanes*. Yet, in spite of that, I sat down and started writing letters to the ones I couldn't speak to in person. I explained to them in a frank and forthright manner what had happened to me. With the exception of one or two people, everyone was gracious, patient and understanding. Many offered to help again, which completely overwhelmed me. They were quite emphatic that if this was another ploy to use them, they might actually think about killing me, but if I was sincere, then they were willing to give me one more chance. Not bad, considering the majority of them were lawyers.

In order to change my view of money, I had to make a decision that I could no longer seek out investment money from individuals. That was always the money that got me in trouble, and it just did again with my company. My decision was to only go to the people who finance the work I do. In other words, I would only go to broadcasters or studios to finance my projects. No more private money.

I also had to look at my spending and saving patterns. Where had we gone wrong in our personal finances? We were constantly in debt and had unsecured creditors. I had to stop using credit cards. That almost killed me. I still have them today, but I will only use them for business, or when I know we can pay them off in full. Well, let me be totally honest. Recently, I've been putting small amounts on them again, and I recognize that's a guaranteed way to fall back into old habits.

So, we had to stop going into debt, and we had to start watching our spending. My ex-wife Deb should get a lot of credit here, as she was the responsible one, and she created a spending plan. We began keeping track of how much money each one of us spent in a given month. When you're not conscious of that fact, it is unsettling how much money you can waste on inconsequential spending. I'm still using these spending plans today, and I do my weekly numbers to watch my spending.

I still have a difficult time keeping track of my spending at times, especially when we get busy, as I just did on two big productions—*The Gangster Next Door* and our *Yonge Street* miniseries. But since I started to do that, I've been able to get out of debt—that is, to stop going further in and, with the exception of my old creditors from when I was single, I have very few unsecured creditors. A mortgage is secured because the bank can take the house if we don't pay. A car is secured because it has value and acts as collateral.

I've noticed that discussing money when I was married was probably the most difficult task we took on. I hated it. It made me totally uncomfortable. Yet, when I surrendered my finances to God, when we were willing to be changed at depth in this area, then changes started to take place.

When Deb and I met, I was a high-flying divorcee. Without knowing anything about me, she started a relationship, and we moved in together. We had a son, Brendan, within a year. My old behavior was unacceptable. I knew I needed help because of all the issues out of my past. I sought out professional help. When I prayed and asked for guidance, changes began to happen. Once again, the same old pattern that had been present in my other issues, like anger, began to come to the forefront. Deb and I suffered from what we called *divorce head*. Whenever we would get in one of our fights over money, one of us would say, "That's it. I'm out of here. I want a divorce."

The trouble is, neither one of us actually wanted one at that time, but we both had patterns of running when things weren't working out. So we started to look for help. We did couple's work. We did communications training. We did marriage counseling, and all of those activities became the building blocks of a much richer and more patient and forgiving relationship and marriage. While we did actually get a divorce, probably ten years after we started this process, it was not finances that were at the root of it. It was just time for us to move on, and we were able to do that in a mutually loving and supportive way, and I'm sure she would say the same thing.

In Harville Hendricks's book, *Getting the Love You Want*, he points out some very simple exercises that I find are good to do. I tell the woman in my life today, Kathy, at least once a day that I love her. I try and do something nice for her every day. In my case, it is cleaning the kitchen or making her coffee in the morning. I know she likes that. I am able to mirror her in serious discussions, so she knows I'm listening. I acknowledge her feelings as legitimate, and I don't invalidate her when she feels a certain way.

I had the pleasure of meeting Prince Edward a few years ago, and one day at a meeting in Cannes during the television market, I was kidding him about his upcoming marriage. I said, "Do you want to hear what's worked for me in my life?"

He nodded his head between bites of his meat pie.

"Once a week, help with the dishes."

He looked up at me, somewhat reticent, and I shook my head and said, "You've never done a dish, have you?"

"Not too often," was his reply.

"Well, then once a week, you should help with the laundry," I said.

Once again the same sheepish grin crossed his face.

"You've never really done laundry either?"

Apparently not. However, it doesn't matter whether you're the Prince of England or a simple writer, producer, professor or candlestick maker. We all need to do our part in relationships, and Harville Hendricks's books point out the most practical and simple tools for getting one's relationship right.

Kathy brings me lovely little notes and writes positive affirmations for me. She buys me chocolates, she reads lovely pieces from books she's reading and sends me beautiful good-morning emails when I am at home in Canada and not with her at the house in California. She gives me comfort when I feel nervous about our future. I try and support her in her work. Kathy is a remarkable woman, who really does want to be of service and allow people in her area to have choices in how they make a living.

If I didn't release my relationship and my attitudes about relationships to God—if we both didn't believe in some form of a Higher Power—I'm certain our relationship would never last. When we asked to be changed at depth, we are asking to for help to do some very heavy and dramatic work. I'm clear that, whenever I want to change, all the forces of nature and my unconscious go to work, trying to get me to undo that decision. Change is hard. Change is challenging. Being changed at depth is damn near impossible, unless you do have the help of a higher power or God.

One of the key ingredients of the Master Mind principle is to belong to a Master Mind Group. I had one in Toronto, and I'm now doing one in Kingston, Ontario, with two friends. Our one friend Bill, who was a retired psychiatrist, died last year and we brought in another friend who was interested in trying to grow himself. He is a man who has achieved a great deal of material success and has all the outward manifestation of his success, the cars the yachts, and now is seeking to find added value to his life. To do that, we had to find like-minded people whose goals were similar to ours. We originally found five men. What we have in common is our desire to change and be changed at depth. Today there are three of us left, and we may bring in someone else.

I've known these men for a number of years. But I like them all. It's important for me to have like-minded people, because God uses these people: *when two or more are gathered, then I am there too.* It is here where I can utilize the support of my Master Mind Group to change. I want to emphasize again—it is God as you understand God to be. There is no theology involved here. We support one another in achieving our goals. I can be open and honest and share very intimate and personal details of my life, because I trust these men. It is imperative to find others who share your beliefs. It not only helps in a practical way, but in ways we can't see at first, it gives us support. There is strength in numbers, especially in the area of spirituality. However, in my original group, one of the men said to me one day, "your life is too big for me. I don't want to be your friend anymore. You are too self centered" or something to that effect. That statement shocked me. As I thought about what he had said, I looked to see if there was any truth in it and I realized, he was really just talking about his own issues and in fact, it had nothing to do with me.

And once again I had to learn, not everyone is perfect and I really can't take anything personally. So, it's important to remember that we are all fellow travelers and that none of us are perfect. And not everyone will remain our friend for life. People and circumstances change and I must be prepared to accept this and change with them as well.

It is important to read spiritual material to help me change. I need to feed my mind as I feed my body. If I don't take the time to nurture my intellect and emotions, then I will suffer from spiritual malnutrition. It is necessary for me to constantly keep looking for whatever inspirational material is out there. Whether it is listening to tapes by Marianne Williamson, or reading her books, or listening to Jack Boland's tapes, I have grown tremendously. Whether it's reading Deepak Chopra, Harville Hendricks, Scott Peck's *The Road Less Traveled,* or reading the Bible, we have to give our souls sustenance.

I highly recommend visiting or joining a church. There are fabulous churches all over the world. I believe it is good for all of us to visit alternative faiths to help us understand one another. What becomes abundantly obvious in a short time is how much they all have in common, not how different they are.

If church is not for you and you are serious about change, then there are a number of spiritual fellowships that may meet in a church, but have no religious affiliation. You may be suffering from any one of the dozens of addictions and maladies that are treated by the various twelve-step programs. All of those technologies of transformations have the same goal: to help anyone undergo significant and lasting personality change at depth.

Chapter Fourteen
I Forgive—Step Five

I forgive myself for all my mistakes and shortcomings. I also forgive all other persons who may have harmed me.

WHEN I STARTED WRITING this book, I was acutely aware that I needed to forgive myself for some horrendous mistakes I'd made early in my life, and that there were many people in my life I had to forgive. I had to forgive myself for having blown one of the greatest opportunities a human being could ever have in life—with my original family, and then my producing career. To this day, I don't honestly know why I did what I did with my first children. It's what I thought was right at the time, because I was in so much pain emotionally. When I was twenty-five years old, I thought I needed a new start. That's why I headed out west to start a new life. Unfortunately, it took quite a few years for me to recognize that what I had done, as far as my children went, was a mistake. I shouldn't have left them. Period. That is one of the facts I have to accept today and forgive myself for.

When I was thirty-five years old, I was at the zenith in my professional career, but my personal life was a total disaster. We were so hot, there was nothing that should have or could have stopped me, except myself. I had everything one could hope for in business. We had world recognition for our work in film. We had the respect of our peers, as well as the International Press, who nominated us for two Golden Globe awards in 1983. We had successfully raised millions of dollars for our various productions. We could essentially get a meeting with anyone we wanted to in Los Angeles in the mid to late 80s.

Then I allowed my drug addiction to take over. I sabotaged myself and ruined a golden opportunity. Yet, I couldn't understand why I was operating the way I was.

I couldn't or wouldn't accept that I had a disease. I couldn't accept that I was allergic to anything that was mood-altering. I had a condition that was similar to type two diabetes. Whatever mood-altering substance I ingest set off a pattern of mental and physical craving that nothing could control, until I accepted I was powerless and asked God to help me.

I had to forgive my father for his actions when he was drunk and assaulted my mother and me. I had to forgive him for the horror of my childhood and the ongoing violence I lived with. I had to forgive him for abandoning me as a child. I had to forgive my mother for leaving me alone with him when I was so young. I knew that if I didn't forgive them, then there was no way I could forgive myself.

Anger and resentment are analogous to terminal cancer. They will eat at us until we either kill ourselves—literally or figuratively—or those closest to us. We become poisoned. We become victims. We literally lose our lives over another human being. They move in and live rent-free in our heads. We cannot shake loose of the wraps that hold us in bondage to the feelings of injustice. Does it mean we sit back and allow people to continue abusing or misusing us? No! We take responsibility for our feelings, and we take constructive steps to break free of the emotions of anger, of resentment and of wanting to get even.

Earlier, I said having resentment and wanting to get even is like you drinking poison yourself, and waiting for others to die. It is one of the great paradoxes of life. Christ said, when he was asked how many times we should forgive, seven times? He said, "Seven times seventy."

We cannot stop forgiving, regardless of how much we've been harmed. As a matter of fact, the more we have suffered, the greater the need to forgive. Why? Because it will allow us to walk into the sunlight of the spirit and break free of the toxic feelings of shame, blame and hatred. And breaking free, like all the other steps we've looked at, is no easy task. But what are the payoffs? Peace of mind, for starters: a sense that I no longer need to focus on people's injustices to me. I can let them go and feel good about myself.

There is such great freedom in letting go of these negative feelings. When we do, we are overwhelmed with a sense of happiness and joy. The fact is, when I'm free of anger and resentment, it is like being reborn again.

Another important element of forgiveness is a sense of acceptance for myself, because I know I have hurt others, too. Not intentionally, but Jack Boland often talks about the conscious and subconscious mind, and how they impact us. Quite often I'm not aware of why I am operating the way I do. My actions are often hurtful and judgmental, because that's how I've operated most of the time. I am a very grumpy guy a lot of the time. I don't mean to be, I just am. My kids have pointed it out to me time and time again.

I am shocked when I find out someone is actually upset with me for being grumpy. I actually don't believe I'm that way. But my unconscious rationalizes my behavior and reinforces that it's okay for me to yell or gossip about someone, because I'm doing it for his or her good. It's not good for anyone. I do not believe there is such a thing as constructive criticism. It is abuse, plain and simple, under a blanket of rationalization. I'm better than you—I really know what's wrong with you and what's best for you. BS. The fact is, I don't know what's good for me half the time. It is a form of spiritual superciliousness for me to assume I know what is good for you, or anyone else. But my mind still tells me, "Can I ever help you out, honest!"

It is my subconscious mind attempting to help me or justify my own position. The trouble is, it is often trying to resolve problems with inaccurate information. What is ironic to me about the subconscious mind is that, if I do ask it to help me—that is, before I go to bed at night, I say something like, "I have this problem. I don't like Harry because Harry has just cheated me out of money, or he's run off with my wife. What is my lesson? What am I to learn? Please guide me to find the right or appropriate answer."

I can assure you that the majority of the time, if I continue this process over and over, I will get the right answer. It might be a hunch or intuition. Or I might find myself led to someone or an event where all of a sudden, I hear what I needed to hear to resolve the problem. There is a caveat here, however: I may not like the answer.

So, what is the first step to forgiveness? I have to be willing to pray for those who've hurt me and—here's the kicker—I have to be willing to have them obtain everything I could possibly ever want in my own life. Oh Lord, this is hard to do, especially when the black-hearted bastards deserve all of the possible plagues, illnesses and demons that God or nature could deliver unto them. But today, I know this is not the right prayer. With God's help, I know I'm able to release whatever anger or resentment is left to him/her, and I am given the ability to forgive those I need to forgive.

As I wrote earlier, I recently had as good an excuse as I'll ever have to hate someone I was in business with. I had to wish these individuals all the success in the world with the company I formed. I was bereft of reason at the very thought of them.

But, as I also noted, I ultimately was responsible for how I handled it. It took me almost six months to forgive them. I was filled with such rabid feelings it consumed me. I couldn't sleep for several months. And that's when I knew I had to do something constructive, because I was suffering. I had to start praying. I had to be willing to let them be successful and to enjoy their lives. It was so difficult, because I was possessed by negative feelings. And what's at the root of it? Pride. Self-centered pride. I was jealous, too. And underneath all of that is hurt and betrayal.

I want to emphasize again, when I don't get what I want, or I lose or may lose something I have, that becomes the chief activator of these negative personality traits that cripple me.

I have to be bigger than the situation. What is remarkable to me is how, when I am able to do it, I start to experience real peace, real serenity. And then the big payoffs start. I am able to forgive myself for many of the mistakes I've made in the past. While I'm not one who subscribes to Eastern religions, I do believe they contain a great deal of truth. One of the most prominent truths that they contain is the Law of Karma.

When I looked back in my life, I saw that I had really betrayed several of my partners, particularly when I was in active addiction. When I sat down one night and realized that what had just happened to me is what I did to others all those years ago, it was like a giant light bulb went on in my head. Think of the image in the old Ford commercials from the 1970s, with the light bulb. I did that. It's as if all of a sudden, I realized that the karmic debt I owed for my actions in the past had just been cleared away.

Now all that was left was monetary. I'd cleaned away all of the unhealthy and mean-spirited actions on my part from all those years ago, when I'd been ruthless in my business dealings. Now I knew how all the people I'd harmed had felt. It was a moment of clarity. I was able to forgive more than I ever could have imagined.

Taking responsibility for our lives and the way they turn out is very liberating. We are responsible for the way we handle difficulties. At least in the Western world, our adversaries generally only harm us emotionally and financially. It puts things in perspective when I look at the justice meted out by the Taliban in Afghanistan, or the Khmer Rouge all those years ago in southeast Asia, where they tortured and murdered millions of people whose points of view differed from their black or white thinking.

Once again, I have peace in my life. I have a sense that all is well in the universe and I will end up where I am supposed to, regardless of myself. As I said, I don't know what is good for me or anyone else. It's not my job to know. It's almost like life is none of my business. In other words, when I trust my Higher Power, I don't need to know the results. I have to have the faith that it will work out, and it usually does. Never quite in the way I'd expected it to, but it does work out.

If I'm not able to forgive, then I live my life filled with poison. I am so overwhelmed by negative thinking and feelings that nothing works out. I'm no fun to be around. People walk the other way when I show up. I have nothing to give in a relationship, because everything is about me. I'm consumed with self. But when I can forgive and I can let go, I am given a new lease on life. I create room for others, and I have compassion. And people like people with compassion. Compassion breeds love and respect. One of the prayers I've used extensively from Catherine Ponder's book is: *Christ in me is my releasing Power. Christ in me is my forgiving Power. Christ in me now frees me from all resentment or attachment toward or from people, places, or things of the past or present that are no longer part of the Divine Plan for my life. Christ in me manifests my true place with true people and the true prosperity now.*

It is truly wonderful to be released from these feelings of anger and hurt. It gives you back your life. It allows you to wake up in the morning filled with joy again. But what about the people we've hurt? If you're human, then trust me, regardless of how little you think you've hurt or harmed others, there will be a swath of individuals from our lifetimes that we have harmed or hurt.

I had to begin praying and affirming that I was being forgiven by the people I'd harmed—emotionally, sexually or financially. I had to go back in my life and realize that I'd taken advantage of women when I was single and didn't really care about their well being. I just wanted to be satisfied physically—disregarding how they felt emotionally.

I've had to ask God to help me forgive myself for introducing a couple of women to cocaine. I know that it caused them serious harm in their lives. I only did it a few times, but I deeply regret it. It didn't serve them at any level. I never had to force anyone to do it. They all did it willingly, but I'm just saddened by the fact I had to have anything to do with it, at any level during my life. However, like the great Catholic saint, St. Augustine, I did identify with his precept, "Lord, make me chaste, but just not right now," which was my motto at that time.

I know that I had to be forgiven by my family for the times I'd never shown up, or lied to them about what was going on with me. It was not easy facing my brothers or sisters, and especially my firstborn children.

I've tried to explain my illness to my son, using this analogy. It's not an excuse for my behavior, but it might help him or my daughter understand where I was—physically, emotionally and spiritually.

How would you feel if someone had a rare form of brain tumor, or mental illness, and their actions were reprehensible while they were sick? Would you hate them, or forgive them? Most people always say, " I'd forgive them, of course."

I suggest to you that if you are in a home with an alcoholic/drug addict or someone suffering from the disease of addiction—whether it is gambling, sex or food, and especially food—about the only one that I seemed to have missed, then I pray you can see these people as sick and in need of your sympathy and prayers.

As I said, this is not to release them from the responsibility of their actions or just excuse them. But what they have is an illness, recognized by the American Medical Association. Addiction is perhaps the most insidious disease known to humankind because we, who are addicted, are the architects of our own adversity. We have no one to blame but ourselves. Yet, most of us live in denial about it. We think we can stop ourselves. Occasionally, very occasionally, some can, but the number is so infinitesimal, it is hardly worth mentioning. The vast majority of alcoholics/addicts go to their graves prematurely because they can't accept they have a medical condition that is not curable, but can be arrested one day at a time.

When I was in the midst of my active addiction, I was completely impervious to the pain I was causing others. When I was able to get it, I really saw the hurt on their faces. And I'd always thought the only one I really hurt was myself. I am so grateful to my oldest brother, who was able to help me so much on my way back.

When it came to my creditors, I felt total embarrassment. I still do at times. Yet, I affirmed through God's grace that I was being forgiven for the harm I'd caused them. This is the one that I am still working through. After *Dixie Lanes*, I would receive the most abusive and harassing calls imaginable. I was called a loser, a scumbag, and puke.

I used to hang up from these calls from collection agencies and former associates, and sit down in a state of emotional shock. There were times when I broke down alone and cried. I had no idea what to do. I was so overwhelmed by the amount I owed. I didn't want to owe this money. I didn't consciously want to screw up my life. The fact is, before *Dixie Lanes*, I'd always paid my investors and creditors.

That's how the idea for this book was born. But I also knew I needed some time under my belt, so there would be some credibility to what it was I was saying. When I first thought of doing this, I was about five years abstinent from drugs. Very respectable, but I was still susceptible to the same flaws, and I knew I needed to change the basic character traits before I could speak with any authority about them. Now I'm in my twenty-fifth year of being clean. I believe that qualifies me to write as I am with some knowledge of the outcome, recognizing that there is still room for significant improvement.

To me, one of the greatest hurdles I've had to overcome is my selfishness. I know I am still selfish. But I know if I'm to truly be forgiven and learn to forgive myself, I must continue on the path of finding the right answer in this area. When I am able to forgive others for the harm they've done me, I am in turn forgiven for the mistakes I've made. It allows the universe to help us out—to find a solution to our dilemmas.

What has become abundantly clear to me is that fundamentally, we are all the same. Yes, there will be about five percent of the population that will have their affairs in order, and will become self-sufficient regardless of what happens with the economy. The vast majority of us, however, are not that lucky. We need to find a way to forgive others and ourselves. We need to be able to work and live in harmony, or else many of us will find ourselves out on the street, cold and hungry.

It was at my Master Mind Group in Toronto and Oakville that I was able to do my original work on forgiving my business partners. Week after week, I would ask to be able to forgive them. Then I would revert to hating them and wishing they would arrive in Heaven, very prematurely. It is so important for all of us to have someone we can talk to about these issues. My Group gave me a safe place where they wouldn't participate in gossip, but only in constructive work, so I could get over the resentments I had and get on with my life.

It was interesting to watch Richard Gere get booed off the stage in New York City at the huge benefit concert for the victims of 9/11. He was the only one who acknowledged that healing was needed. What's funny is how many of the victims themselves have talked about forgiveness. The wife of the young man that prayed with the cell phone operator talked about it. Yet, the participants that evening couldn't or wouldn't hear about it.

However, we all need to forgive Bin Laden and his cohorts, or we become like them. Vengeance is unhealthy. Justice is appropriate. It may even mean the death penalty in some places, although I personally don't agree with it. It gives them martyr status. Thirty to sixty years in a nine-by-nine-foot cell gives you a lot to think about.

Forgiveness is the key to happiness. Forgiveness is the key to a useful life. Forgiveness is essential if we are to move on in our lives. You may have been sexually abused. You need professional counseling, no matter what anyone says. Yes, God can heal it, but God also uses people to help us heal. Religion alone is not enough. Spirituality alone is not enough. But it is an intricate piece of the puzzle in putting our lives back together again.

Forgiveness sets us free—free of hatred, free of fear and free to love again. I suggest it is impossible to truly love if we have resentment in our lives. It's just not possible. God loves us regardless of what we've done. Too bad we don't love ourselves so easily. Self-forgiveness is the greatest gift you can give yourself.

Chapter Fifteen
I Ask—Step Six

I make known my specific request, asking my partner's support, in knowing that the Higher Mind is fulfilling my needs.

BY NOW, it should be apparent to you that the best way to work these steps is with one or more people. I read in the literature and heard in his tapes that Jack had a number of Master Mind partners. It's okay to have more than one Master Mind group, in his opinion. One might be with your spouse or significant other. One might be with your kids. One might be like the one I have here in Kingston, with some like-minded men. I have also participated in an online Master Mind/Master Mind Group who are primarily in the United States. They are wonderful people, and each week as we put our requests out there, they respond with love, wisdom and kindness. That group is split evenly between men and women.

You can state your purpose in these groups. Whether it's to help you develop a deeper, more meaningful marriage or relationship, or to guide you in matters of business or spirituality, it really works best if we're working it with someone else.

Remember what Jesus said: "When two or more are gathered in my name, I am there also."

When I forget to ask for help in my relationship, or when I think I can do it on my own, that's when I really get into trouble. It's not a wise move on my part. When I let my mind take over, I'm almost always guaranteed to screw up whatever it is I'm about to undertake. I have a mind that should have a little sign around it: "Dangerous neighborhood. Do not enter alone. Watch for falling toxic ideas."

The other significant area I find a challenge (which would be any time it comes up) is money. As I wrote earlier, budgeting, spending, saving, having or not having, are all hot buttons for me. There was a time, before I sought spiritual help, when I would go completely crazy in my thinking. That generally would last about an hour, and then I would start to think, "Hold on. What is the one common denominator that is present in all my financial issues? Me!" This led me to begin investigating why I had the attitude I did about money. It was, in my opinion, a learned behavior. My father was my role model, and not a good one. However, my mother turned her life around, and I began to investigate what can I do to change my attitude about money. I sought out answers and found them. Today, I am very conscious about money. I save money and have savings. I have a plan to repay my creditors, and I try not to use unsecured credit today. I keep track of my spending and I keep track of my numbers. I have not had a financial crisis in over ten years. When I am conscious, when I ask for help and guidance with my finances and ask for solvency, I am led to the best possible outcome.

After my divorce, I thought, no more relationships.

So, there I was in Los Angeles at the airport, and I'd been divorced and separated for five years. In that time, I'd met one woman whom I really felt very strong emotions for. However, there were family issues there that were insurmountable for me. So, after that brief encounter, I thought, I'm not investing this kind of energy or time into another one. It's taken me so long to get to where I am, that I just wouldn't want to go through it again. Having to get to know someone's idiosyncrasies, habits, likes and dislikes—what she likes in her coffee, what she wants for dinner when she's tired and grumpy.

So much for that thought, because we all know about the best-laid plans—there is a Chinese saying, and I paraphrase: "The gods laugh while we make plans." So, there I was, and I started chatting with a very nice woman who was also travelling. I thought she was married, so it was quite casual. I was with my friends and associates from Toronto and we were shooting our series, *Yonge Street, Toronto Rock & Roll Stories*—and we were on our way to New Orleans to interview one of the musicians who would appear in the show. When they called my flight to Texas where we're connecting onto New Orleans, I said goodbye and wandered onto the airplane. When we landed in Houston, I walked over to the gate where the flight to New Orleans was, and there she was again. I got excited. I asked her if she was going to New Orleans too, and she said, "Yes, we're going," and she pointed to another gentleman standing some distance off. I was disappointed and said, "Great. Well, I hope you have a wonderful trip," and started down the jet way toward some of the crew I was traveling with.

One of my friends and associates, Jan, said, "Who's that?" I explained, and he glanced at Kathy and said, "She's not married." I dismissed his observation and walked toward the aircraft. Jan wandered over and asked her if she was married, and she tells me she was caught off guard. As it turns out, she wasn't and in fact, the man was her business associate.

So, out of the blue, here I am sitting in northern California editing this book. And who am I with? Kathy, who I met that day in the Los Angeles airport. And boy, am I ever happy. You can't imagine.

Since then, I've asked every day to be guided to the best possible relationship for both of us, and that we are able to live together harmoniously. One of our challenges is that I live in Canada and Kathy lives in northern California. So, I am praying for the guidance on how to best utilize my time, so I am able to spend the maximum amount of time with her and still be responsible for my business. When we do that, and I take the time to pray and ask for help in our relationship, all sorts of wonderful things happen.

One of the best decisions that I've ever made was to move to the country. When I was married, we talked about it for over ten years. Now I wonder, what took us so long? Before I started Master Minding, I used the concept of 'picturing,' which works well with the Master Mind principle.

I put pictures on a large sheet of Bristol board. About twelve years ago, I cut out pictures of a bungalow overlooking water. Today, I have a bungalow on the crest of a small hill, overlooking the Bay of Quinte. Seeing what you want, being crystal clear about what you want, can really help the process of obtaining whatever it is you desire out of life. If you want a car, get a brochure of that car and place it on your Bristol board. This is a private matter, and it is between you, your Higher Power and your group partners. Don't take it out to show it to your friends. They make think you've lost your mind, but trust me: you'll have found it.

Do you want good health? Put a picture up of when you were healthy and ask for it. Write out an affirmation that *God is supplying you with perfect health, wealth and understanding*, then bring your request to your partners. Do you want to travel to exotic locations? Get a travel brochure and have your destination up on the board, too. I want a 28-foot Viking sailboat. There's one down the road from us. I'm going to get a picture of it somewhere in the next few weeks and put it on my new board for 2012. When I write out my goals and put them on a board, and then bring them to my Master Mind partners, I generally accomplish most of them.

This year, I'm really going after my big ones. I want this book to be a success. That is, it will generate talks and revenue for me that will help pay off the last of the creditors from that $4 million of debt, which is less now than $200 thousand. But I have to be specific. Does it have to be a traditional literary success? No. If people buy it and find it useful, then it is a success. If one person out there is able to utilize something I've learned somewhere else, and it helps them, then this book is a success. If I am able to pay off some, all, or the majority of my old creditors, then this book is a success. It will be a matter of degrees of success. I will write on a piece of paper and have it beside a picture of me with the words: "Debt free and happy."

It works well to imagine whatever it is you want, whether it's a new relationship, a new house, a new car, or a new career. Put whatever it is you want on paper, and then declare it to your Master Mind partner/s. It helps to be very specific. Then, let go of the results. I will expand on this point in the next chapter.

Here, I have to take into account that whatever I desire must also be in my best interests for the greatest good for all involved. If I want something that will create a negative result, then chances are it's not going to work. If I hate my former partner and I ask my Master Mind to get him for me, then it's not going to work. Or, I may want to beat someone out in business because of ego. Chances are, that's not going to work. If I want to steal someone's girlfriend or wife, it is not likely to happen. So we must be aware of what it is we are asking for, and how it might be of value to those around us, too. Our requests are to be for our greatest good, and as I said, I often don't know what is good for you or me. So I trust my higher power to only create situations where I can learn and benefit others. *This or something better, God, let thy will be done.*

I really do love my house in the country, and Kathy's in northern California. I sit each morning, coffee in hand, appreciating it. My daily inspirational books, my journal and I spend between half an hour and an hour a day getting ready to meet the world.

I am trying to be a good partner today. It is good to contribute an equal effort to our relationship. When I share the load fifty-fifty and don't walk around in a constant state of expectancy, it's amazing how good life is. Old ideas die hard, slow, painful deaths.

When Kathy decided to give up her position at her work, we talked about her concerns: how will she survive? She might not have enough, unless she takes a traditional 9-to-5 job. But that might get in the way of our ability to travel back and forth between our two residences.

Quite often, people's minds will automatically go to a default setting, just like a computer. "We'll be busted and disgusted." The fact is, whenever I've prayed for guidance and asked for help, it's always been fine so far. In my case, when I moved to the country, I was able to keep working as a writer/producer. Our kids don't have scurvy or rickets. There's gas in the cars and hey, I still have two cars. The lights are still on, as is the heat. I'm doing pretty well, I think.

So, how do we find a way to have it so Kathy can have what she wants, and I can do what I want? The one word in the world that was always a challenge to me is compromise. The more I practice it, the better my life is.

So, what do I do about money? So far I've been able to keep writing and producing, and that has met my needs. Do I have everything I want? No. I want a Porsche—just one, before I shuffle off the planet. In tough times like last year, I was able to utilize some of my savings, because I had made changes over a decade ago that saw me put away a reasonable amount of money for my retirement. This year was much better, and we are working toward being debt-free by the end of this year. Then, using the principles I've acquired, I have a priority list on my old debts from 1986.

It helps to have a partner who shares your belief, so we can take chances in life. Too many people are afraid to step out in faith and try anything. What about the pension? What about the benefits? Who cares? We're only here once—you might as well go for the gusto. What's the point of playing for the pension, getting to sixty-five and finding out eighteen months later you have lung cancer, heart disease or have a stroke? Live for today, and live as if it is your last day on earth. One of these days it will be, and we might as well get as much living in as we can. We don't have a lot of time to waste here on earth. The whole economic meltdown of the last few years has eviscerated people's pensions at companies like Nortel where employees thought they would have it all. Same with auto manufacturing. There are no guarantees in life except that we will all face difficulties at some point in our lives.

I believe if we try to be of service in our occupations and ask for guidance, we will be taken care of. In thirty years of being self-employed, I've never missed a meal. Yes, I've had financial difficulties. But with financial planning and a business plan, regardless of how simple, with stated goals that are written out, keep track of your spending and earnings. You will never go broke if you have more coming in than going out. But, ensure you have money set aside for yourself every two weeks. It's important as well to be able to take time off and give yourself important necessities: a holiday every year and some basic luxuries, like entertainment, travel, a car and a nice home. In my case, I've never ended up on the street. Our needs were always met. Not all of my wants, but a lot of them. And never quite in the way I expected them to be, but my needs were always met.

So I support Kathy in her desire to break free from her traditional employment. I willingly help create the opportunity for her to experience creative and emotional prosperity in her life. When I step out in faith for her, it supports my own efforts, too. This book may never get published. No one may ever read it, other than an agent I know in New York, and a few friends. Every publisher I send it to may reject it. But, for me, I've already experienced significant payoffs from working on it. I've healed the past to a degree I never thought possible.

"What if the critics are unkind to me?" is a thought that goes through my mind from time to time. Of course, that's quite an optimistic view that it will get reviewed. But it wasn't written for the critics—although if one does read it, hopefully they will see the validity and authenticity in it for what it is. It was written for people who might be looking for an answer that I have some experience with. I know it's not a literary masterpiece, and it wasn't written to be one. It's simply me sharing with you, whomever you may be, what it is that's worked for me through the various stages of my life. No big deal. But I do know I've been able to do a lot in life. I know my experiences have real value. I sincerely hope that people who might pick it up, for whatever reason, will read it in the spirit it was written. God only knows what your reaction will be. The results are out of my hands. I've done the best I can.

With my men's group, we get together once a week at a restaurant. Originally, my group met in homes when we were doing it in Toronto and Oakville. But in the country, with us living outside the city, we all head to one central location. Early on, we were lucky enough to find an Anglican church where they were very supportive of our idea. We all threw a few dollars into the hat each week, and we gave it to the church. You might want to start it out that way.

Every week, the three of us meet, with five to ten minutes each to share about our week. Then we ask for what it is we need or desire. We all have families. We all have careers or new business opportunities. We pray for peace of mind, humility, clarity of thought, and guidance in all our business affairs. We all wish to be successful in our endeavors. We all wish to be more connected to our Higher Power. We all want to be better partners, husbands, fathers, brothers and members of society.

In my case, I am desirous of a new career where I can be of service to others. That might mean continuing producing, or it might mean inspirational speaking, wherever and whenever I get the chance. I know I enjoy meeting people, and I know I have a gift for speaking. The challenge for me is to trust that my prayer is being answered. I've been asking for almost ten years for this change. It's funny how my priorities around producing have changed. I've done it for so long that I know, no matter what I do, it won't really have any great impact on my life—with either success or failure. I know I've done good work too. Especially around *The Gangster Next Door, Yonge Street, Toronto Rock & Roll Stories, The Pagan Christ, Unmasking the Pagan Christ, The Grey Fox*, Around the World with Tippi, *Meeting the Crisis,* based on the 12 Steps, *Life After Death, No Price Too High* and *Counter Force*. But when I did them, I was originally motivated by the work itself, and not the message I was carrying. That's the difference today. I now do projects that have substance to them, and I refuse to do stupid films or television.

I find that I feel somewhat conflicted about asking God for things. I worry I am being too selfish. I've been told that it would be best if I only prayed for God's will. Part of my healing process has been for me to realize it is okay to ask God for help: with my relationship, in my desire to get closer to God, with my career choices, to help me raise the necessary funds to pay off all of my old creditors, to earn enough to meet our needs so we can live comfortably.

It is also okay to ask God to help us with our projects—like *The Lens*, a series created by a young woman, Alyssa Davalos, where we highlight companies that are verging on creating a possible ecological disaster like the BP oil spill. I want to help. I want guidance. I want prosperity. Today, though, I've learned that prosperity means so much more than just money. I want to experience the fullness of life's riches. I want to travel with Kathy, so we can see the wonders I've seen. I want to experience spiritual riches, and I do that by trying to be of service.

I try and help wherever I can, with little regard for the benefit. If I give of my time, I find myself with more time. If I give money, I seem blessed with more money. If I give to the hungry, or help a friend back on his feet, I'm helped in return. If I want to keep something, something I really value, then the best thing I can do is give it away. Paradoxical but true!

One of the prayers and affirmations I use today is: *I am worthy, and I deserve a happy and peaceful relationship and family life. We deserve a nice home, sufficient revenues to meet our needs, and a successful career. I deserve God's love and generosity.*

Every part of me used to experience discomfort when I would say that affirmation. I did not feel worthy when I first started. I did not feel I deserved God's love, or any blessings. But I have changed. Today, it is okay for me to ask God to help me resolve difficulties in my relationships. It is good to ask for help with forgiveness. It is good to ask our Higher Power, God, to bless others. I have prayed often for all those who lost their lives in the World Trade Center, the Tsunami a few years ago in Asia, the earthquake in Japan and also asked that God bless the families and the children. *"Please give them Peace"* has been my prayer. I have done the same for the tsunamis, and all the other natural and man-made disasters. This is one part of the mystery of life I cannot understand. How it is that people suffer—where is God in that?

It is very powerful to have partners with whom we can share our longings. When two or more are gathered, there is definitely a shift in one's consciousness. It is apparent that something quite remarkable is happening. There have been recent studies done in the United Kingdom on cancer patients who've been prayed for by others for a healing. It doesn't matter whether they know it or not, according to this study. Those who've been prayed for experience remissions more readily than those who haven't. There is empirical proof that praying works. Having Master Mind partners, who pray with us and join us in empowering our requests, is a wonderful experience.

I believe the more our prayers and requests are rooted in the spiritual, the more likely they are to be answered expediently. I also believe it is all right to ask our Master Mind for material achievements. I have desires that I mentioned earlier. I have released those requests to my Higher Power, and when the time is right, they will be manifested. I always add, if it be your will. First and foremost in my case are the necessary funds to pay off all the people I feel I have an obligation to from so long ago.

I believe when my requests will help others, I will truly be blessed and helped. It will enable me to reach those goals in record time.

Chapter Sixteen
Give Thanks—Step Seven

I Give Thanks: I give thanks that the Master Mind is responding to my needs, and I assume the same feelings I would have if my request were already fulfilled.

THE ONE WAY I HAVE DISCOVERED to create more of anything in life is to give thanks for what I already have. Too often, people believe they have nothing. All it would take for any Canadian, American or Western European to realize how fortunate we are is to travel to some parts of the world where they literally have nothing. Children are dying by the hundreds every minute of every day in parts of Africa. People live in grinding poverty in India. Children are sold into prostitution to give the family money in parts of Asia. Life is cheap in many parts of the world. Children are murdered every day and every night in some South American countries, to get rid of the begging and stealing problem. Murdered! It is beyond comprehension to me that this goes on in so-called civilized countries, but it does. When I think of how we perceive children here in North America, it is absolutely mind-boggling that society as a whole allows these actions to take place, but it does.

That gives me pause to reflect that, while I may not have a mansion, I do have a warm bed to sleep in, plumbing to relieve myself in private, and hot water to take a bath in. To a great portion of the world, these are unheard-of luxuries. We have a car, as do significant numbers of North Americans. We have public transportation that works and is readily available. Over ninety percent of us have work and can support our families, so they are not starving.

We have so much to be grateful for. Sometimes it is good to make up a gratitude list when we don't think we have anything. Did you eat today? Do you sleep in a bed last night? Do you have a roof over your head, regardless of how humble it is? Do you have a friend or loved one that loves you, too? Do you have work? Do you have an education? Are you in reasonable health? Do you have access to some fundamental health care? Can you practice the religion of your choice? Can you change your social or economic standing by simply making the decision that you want to? These are some very basic questions that a significant portion of the world's population can't answer affirmatively to.

We in the Western world are truly blessed. We can have whatever we want. If you are willing to pay the price, and you're willing to put in the effort, you can create any lifestyle you want. Good or bad. It's your choice. How do you create the lifestyle you want?

I try and take a few minutes out during the day and imagine I have already achieved what I want. I find this easy to do when I am going to bed at night. I see Kathy and me happy, walking along a country road in either eastern Ontario or the beautiful redwoods of northern California. I see my kids' smiling faces because they've succeeded at their work or, in my youngest daughter's case, university has improved significantly. I see my creditors paid off.

We all have imagination. It is a great tool to use. Creation gave it to us for a reason. When we utilize our imagination, we are able to create mental images of what it is we desire. This helps our subconscious mind in guiding us to take the appropriate actions that help us produce the results we desire. It is good to imagine yourself sitting on the beach in Mexico, if that's what you want. Imagine the white sandy beaches, the row upon row of palm trees stretching out for miles and the sound of the waves breaking against the shoreline. Imagine the picturesque haciendas, all painted in pastel colors. Smell the glorious food cooking in the restaurants. Hear the sounds of the Mariachi bands playing at dinner, the voices rising in beautiful melodic harmonies.

Imagine yourself with the person you wish you had a relationship with as you walk down the street. If there's someone you've met and you wish you could go out with him or her, imagine yourself out at dinner. See yourself laughing and relaxing in their company. Here, you are able to imagine that you ask them what they do. What do they like in life? What do they want out of life? What are their favorite activities? Who are their favorite authors, actors, and heroes? What's the single greatest moment or event in their life? When you are interested in others, people will find you interesting.

If you do meet the person and you find out that they have absolutely nothing in common with them, and it's the worst night of your life, give thanks for allowing you to see that this is not the right person to be out with. It's in our attitudes how well we do with giving thanks.

I thank God every morning for another day. I happen to write to God every morning. It's something I started doing quite a few years ago when I was having a problem imagining God, and I wanted a closer relationship with him/her. I was still caught up in my confusion over my Catholicism and whether or not I believed in the divinity of Christ. I started to write God with the idea that he was a friend of mine. It helped me to create a personal relationship with God, though I still don't know who or what God is. I have journal upon journal that I've written with all my letters. Some mornings I'm ranting and raving, but most days I'm simply thanking God for all the blessings I have in my life today.

I often list my requests in those journals, and give thanks that I am being guided to take the right actions. For instance, I have been thinking about the whole process of Master Minding. So here's my latest idea: I could set up seminars for people who want to join in Master Mind groups. Will this work? I have no idea. I could investigate and see if there is somewhere we could host them. Or I could contact Unity churches. I could contact my Catholic church, or the Presbyterian church, and see if they would allow me to use space in the church to hold a seminar.

I begin imagining and seeing myself delivering talks to groups of people. I probably won't fill halls in the beginning, but I might get twenty people out. A few years ago we did a Talking Peace seminar, where we had approximately fifty people attend. It was rewarding, and my only compensation was the good feeling I had that I was able to share my insights into what is going on in the world, because of my experience of creating that Counter Terrorism series. The success was that we had fifty people contemplating the fact that they might be able to make a difference, regardless of the fact I was living on a small island at that time, far away from the centers of influence.

But I had a chance to see that my style of speaking and message got across. Where did I get it from? Before the evening started, I imagined I was being guided in what was said. No one walked out angry or upset. As a matter of fact, some very good ideas came out of the evening, and they want to do more of the talks. All of these experiences are leading to my career as an inspirational speaker and writer.

Another approach is to act as if you already have whatever it is you want. If you want to be a successful salesperson, or a successful commercial artist, a successful writer, a successful physician, a successful mother, a successful husband or parent, a successful auto technician, imagine yourself already in possession of it, and begin acting as if you are already have whatever it is you desire. How would you feel if you'd already received your request? You would feel happy, would you not? You would feel a real sense of accomplishment. You would feel proud of yourself. You might try feeling grateful, too.

When I am home at this time of the year, I can stare over my deck and see the beautiful Bay of Quinte, sparkling blue. All I have to do is think of myself sailing along in my new 28-foot Viking, the Genoa, catching the wind as I release my mainsail. I can feel the wind against my face and the sun warming me. I can hardly wait. I get really excited just thinking about it.

My son Brendan wants to sail more than anything else. He is now taking lessons at a Toronto sailing school. He works with me, and we both love the idea of sailing. Brendan and I used to go to the Yacht Club across the bay from our old house and just hang around. The good news is, my two friends own beautiful sailboats that we can go out on anytime we want. It's one of the gifts of the universe.

Right across from my desk at my house in Sandhurst, and right beside the window looking out over the bay, is a model of a '57 Chevy convertible (right next to the model of a beautiful sailboat). To my right is a copy of the Bob's Big Boy menu from Burbank, California, with a red '57 Chevy convertible on it. The owner of the restaurant gave me one a few years ago when I mentioned I really loved the picture on the cover. I sit and imagine myself driving along in the summer, the top down, listening to good old rock 'n' roll on the radio. Actually, it will probably be classical music that I'm listening to right now.

When I was a young producer and hadn't produced anything yet, people used to say to me, "What do you do?"

"I'm a producer," I would respond.

"What have you produced?"

"I'm working on two projects right now." And I was, too. I'd bought the rights to a novel I found, and I was working with Phillip on *The Grey Fox* and helping with the financing of *Nails*—getting him the money to finish paying off his creditors. That's part of the job of producing. Getting the money. I used to lie in bed at night and imagine having all the money in the bank, but I always acted and spoke as if I was a producer. I did the same thing as a young record producer, too.

When we were making *The Grey Fox*, I used to sit and meditate and imagine having all the money, because we were having such a hard time raising the funds. I imagined the film finished, and I imagined it being successful. I saw us winning awards. I saw newspaper articles in my mind that were very positive.

I stopped doing that for several years, and I found myself back in the desert as a result. However, I recently went back and imagined positive press and critical reviews and awards on *Yonge Street, Toronto Rock & Roll Stories,* and *The Gangster Next Door,* which was the Canadian Broadcasting Corporation's highest-rated documentary for this year, and we were able to get the TV Magazine covers on *Pagan Christ.* When I first started again, I used this on a series we did for TLC and History Television called *Counter Force,* and it happened all over again. We won the Gold Special Jury Award at Houston against twelve hundred other series this year. We received the Christopher Award too, where we competed against over a thousand entries. There are more, but I won't bore you with them. I know that imagining works. When I assume the feelings I would have if what I wanted came to me, then I am guided to take the right actions to accomplish my goals.

The human brain is the world's greatest computer. It will guide you and give you answers, if you just give it the opportunity. When you choose to use your Master Mind partner with it, the analogy is like loading in sophisticated software to really get it working. Our subconscious mind will always guide us and get us the right answer, if we ask it to. That's the voice of God—speaking directly to us.

One way to utilize it is through meditation. Meditation is sitting quietly and listening. Prayer allows me to talk to God and give him my requests, and meditation allows me to sit back and listen for His/Her reply.

When I allow my mind to slow down, to relax and allow all of the thoughts to pass on through, then I open myself up to experiencing the flow of power that comes from a conscious contact with your higher self. Here, we experience directly the feelings we would have if our request were already present. Here we can get in touch with our inner self, our unconscious mind, and allow it to give us the knowledge we need to realize our desires.

If your interest is in pursuing a life in the arts or creativity, I can assure you that it is an amazing experience to tap into the universal unconscious, which the late, great, Pierre Tiehard de Chardin, a Jesuit paleontologist involved in the discovery of the "Peking man," referred to as "Cosmic Consciousness." There exists around the earth a layer of super consciousness, that every human being can tap into and utilize for our highest good to improve our conscious contact with God, and to receive inspiration and extraordinary insight.

It really does allow you to grow and improve your chances of success exponentially. Meditation has several benefits to it. One is the obvious ability to access creativity. Intuition is increased, and we are led toward projects, people and outcomes that support our goals. We find ourselves inexplicably calm, too. We are plugged into a source of power and energy that is always available to everyone, but few take advantage of. Meditation does work to unlock the secrets of the ages as well. We will find ourselves receiving images and ideas that are quite profound and beautiful. The image I have is of a wave of tranquility, washing over us and leaving us refreshed and whole.

When I ask my unconscious for help solving a problem, and then take the time to meditate, I am often given insights into the problem other than the solution. I see how my actions have led me there, and what I might do in the future to avoid the same pitfalls.

I can have visions of my life as I would like it to be. I can see clearly what it is I need to do, to accomplish a desire. I am led to the suitable ideas, people or institutions that will enable and empower me to realize my worthy ideals. When I really believe that God is responding, and I assume the feelings I would have if I accomplished my goal, it's as if I have uncovered a shortcut to my desires. My unconscious cannot tell the real emotions from ones I choose to make up. But it will react to them. When we tell our unconscious that we feel successful, it proceeds to help us attain whatever it is we think or tell it we should have.

My unconscious does not have value judgments like my conscious mind does. It simply enables me to operate in a way that creates what it is I'm really thinking of at that time. That's why, if I harbor negative unconscious thoughts, my life is filled with negative results a great deal of the time. I don't understand why I feel this way. It's because I'm totally unaware that I have these feelings and thoughts, and I'm shocked when I wake up depressed or anxiety-ridden.

Giving thanks ensures more peace, more prosperity, more feelings of satisfaction and more of what it is we are giving thanks for. Giving thanks opens up a channel of receiving. It allows us to access God's grace in abundance. It enables me to expand my positive beliefs and experiences.

It is also important to give thanks when we are facing difficulties. Every obstacle carries with it the seed for equal or greater opportunity. When we are faced with difficult situations, we can either see them as problems, obstacles or challenges. I choose to take the path of a challenge. When I give thanks for the difficulties in my life, I open the door to their solution. Inevitably, there is something I have to learn. I remind you of my story of *Dixie Lanes*. I really thought my life was over. I thought I had to give up California, where I loved living. I had to give up my movie career to get better, which completely devastated me. I had to give up (I thought) who I was. Well, let's look at the reality of it.

The most important realization I had was that, if I'd never come back to Toronto, I would never have met the woman who became the mother of my two youngest children, and who played a significant role in my development as a human being. I would not have the beautiful children I do in my son, Brendan, and my daughter, Laurel. I would not have renewed my relationship with my children from my first marriage, Andrew and Colleen. I probably wouldn't have cleaned up the wreckage of my former marriage, either. I would not have healed the relationship with my mother and my family. I would not have been there to assist my mother in her greatest time of need. You can't put a price tag on that experience, or the healing power of all those elements.

The week I went back to Toronto in 1987, there were about five shootings on the Pacific Coast highway in California. Fires raged through the canyons, and the hills started to all slide into the ocean. Many of my friends had to park four-wheel drive vehicles facing out of the driveways, so they could escape if a really big landslide started. Then they tore down the Malibu Coffee Shop and put up a nondescript mall. That made leaving easier. The fact is, I still visit LA regularly, and I still love all of the wonderful things I can do in southern California. I love LA, as Randy Newman sang years ago, but I'm also happy at home in Canada. Now I have northern California too, an area I never thought I would end up in. And I love it as well.

When I had to give up my movie career, my stress level dropped significantly. I started to sleep after a few months, something I hadn't done in years. I began to realize how unhealthy it was "being" what I did for a living. All of a sudden I went into an incredible depression, because I didn't have my ego identification anymore. Was that ever liberating when I realized I am not what I do for a living.

I have other interests, more than making movies or television. I love reading. I love skiing, I love working with others who are in need of help in their lives. I love teaching. I love writing. I love being a father. I loved being a husband. I loved being a volunteer fireman. I loved working on the Amherst Island Men's Society (AIMS) committee to help bring a museum to the island I lived on for nearly ten years, so others might share in the rich heritage of this community, which is referred to as part of the Loyalist Township. This is where the original inhabitants of New England emigrated after the U.S. War of Independence. Our graveyard dates into the late 1700s. I love learning and growing as a human being. I love traveling. I love exploring. I love a good cause. I love getting to know people.

People where I live couldn't care less whether or not I ever lived in Hollywood, New York, or Timmins for that matter. World-renowned neurosurgeons, writers, artists, former television anchors and really interesting farmers surround me. We have a community of working people who build homes, work on roads and teach at Queens University. I would have missed all of this if I'd stayed in California and never given up my feature film producing. The fact is: I'd probably be dead.

When I switched out of independent feature films to television, I actually started to earn money consistently. Sure, the chance to earn millions wasn't really there unless I hit a home run on a series, but gone were the incredible peaks and valleys. My life became financially manageable. I didn't go another dime into debt, either. I started to come out of debt.

And here's something I'd forgotten from my early career. I really liked making television documentaries and series. I didn't have thirty-five different people with their own agendas telling us what to do. We were left alone, and I actually experienced more creative satisfaction than I ever had. It was fun. Wow, there's a concept. Doing something that's actually fun, instead of going out every day to get the crap kicked out of you emotionally, mentally and physically.

I wouldn't have started teaching at universities, I wouldn't have met all the interesting people I know today. I wouldn't be sitting in this home today, enjoying the peace and tranquility of the country listening to CBC 2, our beautiful national FM broadcaster. And think of this. I thought my life was over as I knew it when I lost everything because of *Dixie Lanes*.

Dixie Lanes gave me my true life back. It enabled me to see just how blessed I was, and what a complete fallacy it is to be totally caught up in a career where you sacrifice life to earn a living. So give thanks for difficulties. They will enable you to change the direction of your life, learn a lesson, and move on in a very positive way.

I want to emphasize that it doesn't mean that I may not go back and produce a feature film again. As a matter of fact, I may this year. But it's not going to define who I am or what it is I'm all about. It will simply be that we are creating entertainment.

Giving thanks allows me to obtain more of life. Giving thanks for what we have enables us to experience God's abundance in all areas of our lives. Acting as if we have already received what we're asking for speeds up the process of getting it. There's an old spiritual axiom that really works: Fake it until you make it. It works. It really does.

Chapter Seventeen
I Dedicate My Life—Step Eight

I Dedicate My Life: I now have a covenant in which it is agreed that the Master Mind is supplying me with an abundance of all things necessary to live a successful and happy life. I dedicate myself to be of maximum service to God and those around me; to live in a manner that sets the highest example for others to follow, and to remain responsive to God's guidance. I go forth with a spirit of enthusiasm, excitement and expectancy. I am at peace.

I CAN HARDLY BELIEVE that we've arrived here at the last of the eight steps. This process started the first week of May 2001. As I write this, it is September 25th, 2011. Ten years. But God supplied me with an abundance of energy and dedication to get this book finished, or nearly finished. Here is the greatest single leap of faith I will take with these steps. Either God is, or God isn't. I choose to believe He is. Then I either am willing to release my life totally to His direction and care, realizing that I will be given everything I need to live a success-filled and happy life, or I will continue living on self-directed willpower that often generates fear and confusion in my life.

Self-reliance does work. We just pay an awful price for it. But if you're one of those individuals who views the way of life I'm suggesting as wimpy, boring, phony, or any of the other views I once held about it, then I simply wish you good fortune. I really want to meet someone who has lived his life totally on self-direction, achieving all his material goals, amassing fabulous riches and lying on his deathbed saying, "I wish I'd spent more time at the office." I don't think that's a success-filled and happy life. It is one full of money and power, but it tends also to be a lonely one. We have to sacrifice so much to gain that material wealth—if that is all we are after. I know the rewards are very short-lived.

I realize there are many very successful people, by the way, who have been able to create a balance—that is, they acknowledge that it is God's guidance and love that has enabled them to be so prosperous, but they also tend to have very balanced lives at home and in their spare time. They create opportunities to contribute back to life. They spend time with their families. They give to their community. They are able to give of their time, money and love. That's the key. What are we giving back to life when we're in the midst of getting so much?

This begs the question: what is a successful and happy life? To me, it is the realization of any worthy ideal. If I want a happy and joyous family life, with enough money to meet our current needs and put away some for savings, then that is a beginning. But what else might there be? Well, what about a deeper, more meaningful relationship with your Higher Power? One where you can absolutely let go of worry about the future. One where you can release your career, your finances, your relationship or your marriage, your children or loved ones to God's care, and not have to give it another thought as far as trying to control, fix or manipulate how it's going to turn out.

When we are able to live peace-filled and happy lives, as the result of what we are doing in our daily lives, we are successful. When our children love us, when we contribute to our communities, we are living happy and successful lives. When we think of the needs of others in a healthy way, not a codependent way, we are living happy and peaceful lives. When we can either donate our time, energy, or resources to helping those less fortunate, we are living happy and successful lives. When you build a birdhouse, a garage or a house that you've always wanted, then you're living a happy and successful life. When you get the car of your dreams, or the boat or the fishing rod you've always wanted, you're living a successful and happy life. When you take time out to speak to someone you would not normally speak to and honestly inquire how they are, and listen to what they have to say, you are really living a successful and happy life.

There is no limit to what you can want and have. Travel, excitement and exploration are all worthy ideals. Education—regardless of what age you are—is a wonderful journey. Trying to learn how to play the violin, piano, or guitar creates a successful life if you can play one tune. To me, that is what we can expect when we dedicate our lives to our Higher Power.

You can expect to have enough. It is God's pleasure to give you the kingdom. All you have to do is ask. It is important to remember, however, that when we ask only for ourselves, it won't be as satisfying. But having a covenant, which is a sacred agreement or contract, enables all of us to obtain peace in our lives. Happiness in itself is not something we can generate. Happiness to me is a byproduct of doing something well. It is the gift that comes with giving. Happiness is achievable when we reach a goal, help a friend, give to the community, or seek God's will in our lives. Peace is created by the absence of fear or conflict. That is achieved when we relinquish our worries and doubts to God. Peace comes when we've done the best we can in any situation and let go of the results. Peace is an unearned gift.

Of course, for most of us, we continually worry about how our lives will work out because, while we want to believe, we may have lingering doubts. That's okay, too. But after a period of time, it becomes evident that when we try and work our lives in agreement with God's plan, life just has a way of working out. It means that we can begin living spiritual lives and, in some cases, we might want to start living a religious life too. But having a covenant with God enables all of us to develop our own personal relationship with God that really supports us in our endeavors.

By now, you'll have noticed that an occasional profanity slips out of my fingers (and I must confess, my tongue, too, from time to time) and I've come to accept that it's okay with God, too. It might not be quite as acceptable socially, but my relationship with God allows me the freedom to be who I really am. Not someone I'm not. I trust that those who get to know me recognize that this is who I am, that in spite of my language, I care deeply for others.

How do I reconcile this with part three of the eighth step, where I set the highest example? I don't think it's my language that God cares about. I think He cares about what is in my heart. Do I want to be of service? Do I have love in my heart? Am I mean-spirited, critical, impatient or judgmental at home? Do I try to find a resolution that works for the greatest good and the greatest number in life's problems? In traffic, when I go nuts and give someone the finger, do I try and get them to open their window and apologize for my behavior? Do I admit readily when I've made a mistake? Can I be forgiving of those who've harmed me? Am I willing to put myself out to help someone that may need my assistance because they are disabled?

To me, these are questions that carry much more weight than my use of language. These are the standards that I believe God holds me to, and that people want to know about the real me. I want to be clear. I believe God loves me in spite of my flaws. I don't believe I will ever have the kind of saintliness of a Mother Theresa. That's why she deserves it and undoubtedly will be sainted. I'm no saint. You can take that to the bank.

But that doesn't stop me from trying to act in a decent way. I just recognize that most of my life will have certain struggles in it. I'd love to believe that all of my imperfections will be removed someday.

It's kind of nice to think of myself as this tranquil, peaceful guy who will sit around dispensing wisdom and knowledge with incense burning, while we sip tea. Those who know me can now get off the floor from laughing. Probably not going to happen, they're saying. But I'm okay with that, because I believe God loves me just the way I am. I dispense love and whatever wisdom I've acquired from my local Tim Horton's coffee shop, where I often find myself in my deepest and most meaningful conversations. I feel sorry for our American friends, for they do not have the temple of serenity that we call Tim's.

The most sincere desire I have today is to be of maximum service to God and those around me. I can't believe I'm writing that, but it is true today. When I work with a Master Mind group week after week, I begin to see the miracles that get manifested in our lives. We see our *asks*, or requests, being granted. We see that we are given the tools to handle difficult situations at home. We are able to be present when our loved ones get sick or die. We are able to contribute in a meaningful way when tragedies like the World Trade Center occur, or our economies melt down, or we get sick ourselves.

I want to tell you about our friend, Bill. Bill was a retired psychiatrist. He had the proto evolution symbol on the back of his car—the one that has a fish and underneath it reads "Darwin," with the fish evolving legs. Bill prayed every week with Richard and me for almost ten years. While he never came to a place of accepting that there was an anthropomorphic being—the big guy in the sky—he did come to see the value of prayer and the value of fellowship. Richard figured out that we had over 600 lunches with Bill. When he was laying in the hospital dying, both Richard and I would go visit him, and we'd sit there and pray with him, and you know, no one knew he was going to go—but when he did, he was very, very peaceful. Odd for a man who was a trained medical scientist; first as a doctor, then an anesthesiologist, then a trained psychiatrist who suggested that while he didn't clearly understand how prayer worked, when he did pray, he just felt better. He was the one who was a power of example for me to pray for humility, clarity of thought and peace of mind. Bill was the most humble human being I've ever known—and one of the most spiritual, in spite of being an agnostic.

When we try to be and are of maximum service to others, we find that we are given the answers to problems that in the past may have totally mystified us. Quite often in life, we find ourselves confronted by interpersonal relations that don't go well. We have mutual friends who participate in gossip. When we find ourselves getting sucked into the vortex of personalities, it is difficult to extract ourselves unless we've taken the high road, right off the top. Here's an example of where our covenant supplies us with the spiritual resolve to not get into this form of character assassination.

One great question I heard from someone about gossip was: "Is what you're about to tell me going to contribute in any significant way to my or another person's life?"

The obvious answer is "No," and it tends to stop people in their tracks. I suppose the way we address the issue with them will have a significant bearing on the outcome. If I shame them for their actions versus pointing out to them with love the potential harm their words may cause, the solution may prove more harmful than the problem. When we choose to help our fellow travelers, we are given a sense of peace and happiness.

We find ourselves elevated above these life-draining experiences. We are of maximum service when we try and act in a positive way.

I used to batter people over the head with the truth, under the mistaken belief I was helping them. There are times, however—and this is where discernment really comes in—when you have to get someone's attention with a 2x4. Generally, when people are self-deluded about a perceived harm done to them, or they believe they are being picked on, when the fact is, it is their own self-centeredness that is really at the root cause of some issue, drastic action is sometimes necessary. It's generally a question of your relationship with them. I find a direct, but loving, statement to use. "I know you believe that you were wronged, but I must tell you that I think your ego is out of control."

You might want to ask their permission to share with them your insight. If they say "No," then back off. Life will give them the same message. It may not be as gentle, however.

Our covenant guarantees that we will be able to survive any difficulty life may throw at us with dignity and grace. There is a real sense of satisfaction and happiness to be gained by being a power of example to people going through adversity. If most of your life you've been someone who has been emotionally out of control, someone people have had to assist constantly, think of the reaction of others when you can be there for them. If we accept our covenant with God, then we are able to support those in need, without needing anything for ourselves. I am reminded of the prayer of St. Francis. This is a great philosophy to live by.

> *Lord, make me a channel of Thy peace, that where there is hatred I may bring love; that where there is wrong, I may bring a spirit of forgive-ness; that where there is discord, I may bring harmony; that where there is error, I may bring truth; that where there is doubt, I may bring faith; that where there is despair, I may bring hope; that were there are shadows, I may bring light; that where there is sadness, I may bring joy. Lord, grant that I may seek to comfort rather than to be comforted; to understand, than to be understood; to love, than to be loved. For it is by self-forgetting, that one finds peace. It is by forgiving, that one is forgiven. And it is by dying, that one awakens to Eternal Life. Amen.*

If I choose to live my life by one simple spiritual belief, then I suppose that this prayer is the one to try and live it by. A number of years ago, when I was working on my codependency, I hated this prayer. I thought it was incredibly unhealthy. It spoke volumes to me about losing myself in others' problems, of not taking care of myself.

As I've grown and changed, I've begun to see the healthy elements of this prayer. Francis was an interesting young man when he entered religious life. He gave up a great deal. He had everything a person could want. He had a good family, good prospects, and wealth. Yet, he yearned to be of service. I see when I am healthy, when I have the knowledge that I can make a difference, when I subjugate my ego, I am given great rewards. St. Francis' prayer really is a recipe for peace of mind and happiness. It is also one of the most difficult spiritual disciplines to try and live by, because it is in complete contradiction to my ego-based existence. But it contains the seeds of true joy.

In March 1970, I lay in a horrible black room and talked to a friend on a telephone because, for the first time, I seriously considered committing suicide. I couldn't get free of alcohol. This friend started to repeat the Prayer of St. Francis with me, and I was suddenly catapulted into the fourth dimension. I had a profound spiritual awakening. To this day, I've never had a drink. I was 22 years old at that time. The problem was not in my alcoholism, however. It was in my faulty thinking. I couldn't surrender my old thinking and my absolute desire to only get what I wanted for me. But I recognized there was power in that prayer. It epitomizes the best in spiritual goals.

I trust today that I am being guided. I feel a sense of excitement about the future. I am filled with a sense of hope that I will be able to be of service to others, and really create some dramatic changes in my life. I expect my life to work out. I expect to be able to do my inspirational talks, and I expect that I will be blessed for my efforts.

In the same way, I expect that I will have to deal with issues from time to time in my life that will cause me great pain and suffering. That's the way life is. I know I will be guided to the right people, places and solutions. *I believe and affirm that I am being guided to the right people, the right opportunities and the right results in my life.* I expect great things in my future. I expect that my children will do well. I expect that I will be able to overcome all difficulties in life with God's help.

I expect to be able to travel with Kathy to Europe, Ireland and Asia. As a matter of fact, I just returned from the south of France, and I met Kathy in London. It was one of the nicest and most enjoyable vacations I've ever had.

I expect that I will receive sufficient funds to repay my old creditors. I expect that most people I've harmed will forgive me, and in turn, I will forgive any who have harmed me.

I expect good health for my family and me. I expect prosperity. I expect to have a peace-filled and happy life. It doesn't matter whether I will ever produce another movie or television show in my life. I will be led to the right people and projects, as long as my intentions are to be of service.

I want to close off this book with a story about pain. I've always wondered why, if there was a God, he would allow people to die and suffer what I perceived to be needlessly. Here's what I've come to realize. I don't know why some people need to die prematurely or suffer, but what I've come to realize is that for some, pain is integral to their growth and eventual transformation.

When my son Brendan was born, he was born with 180-degree clubfeet. The poor little guy was heading north, and his feet were going south. When he was six days old, I had to take him to the Hospital for Sick Children in Toronto. The surgeon told me to hold him down on the large metal examining table as he looked at his feet.

Now here was my newborn son, a week old, and I'm sure that his small, undeveloped brain understood only warmth, being dry and feeding. All he felt was love and comfort. But when I laid him on that table, and the doctor took his little feet and twisted them right around so he could put plaster casts on his legs to help straighten them out, all this poor little baby knew was that he was in agony.

My brain is like little Brendan's when it comes to trying to understand God, or his plan for me, or anyone else. All Brendan was capable of was feeling the pain. He didn't understand the concept of healing. Week after week, I kept bringing Brendan back to that hospital, and week after week, he would scream in agony, and the tears would stream down my face because I loved him so much I wasn't willing to let him go through life physically handicapped. I subjected him to that experience for over six months, and then a very painful operation where they cut his foot from one side to the other so they could turn every tendon in his foot, and put a steel pin through his heel to hold his foot straight. By the time he was nine months old, he could recognize the doorway to Sick Children's Hospital in Toronto, and he would just start to shake and sob. He couldn't understand that he needed the pain to change how his feet were pointing, so that today, he walks and runs normally. No one would ever know, unless I told this story that he was born technically disabled.

Pain is the touchstone of change in our lives. I don't know why I have to endure the pain of life at times. All I know is when I do and it ends, I'm always better off than I was. That will probably be true until the day I die. I don't know why people die in mass numbers in natural catastrophes. I don't know why planes crash into buildings, into the ocean, into homes. I don't know why young children die. That is one of the great mysteries to me. Like Brendan, I just cannot figure it out, but undoubtedly I will one day. Until then, I look forward to each day, and all the amazing adventures and challenges I will face and overcome. I look forward to being able to meet some of you as I trudge the road to happy destiny.

God bless you, and may you find your own path to freedom.

Eight Steps to a Spiritually Fulfilled Life

1. *I Surrender:* I admit that, of myself, I am powerless to solve my problems, powerless to improve my life.

2. *I Believe:* I come to believe that a power greater than myself, The Master Mind of God, can change my life.

3. *I am Ready To Be Changed:* I realize that erroneous self-defeating thinking is the cause of my problems, unhappiness, fears and failures. I am ready to have my beliefs and attitudes changed so my life can be transformed.

4. *I Decide To Be Changed:* I make a decision to surrender my will and life to the care of my Master Mind; I ask to be changed at depth.

5. *I Forgive:* I forgive myself for all my mistakes and shortcomings. I also forgive all other persons who may have harmed me.

6. *I Ask:* I make known my specific requests, asking my partner's support, in knowing that our Master Mind is fulfilling my needs.

7. *I Give Thanks:* I give thanks that my Master Mind is responding to my needs, and I assume the same feelings I would have if my request were already fulfilled.

8. *I Dedicate My Life:* I now have a covenant in which it is agreed that my Master Mind is supplying me with an abundance of all things necessary to live in a manner that sets the highest example for others to follow and remain responsive to God's guidance. I go forth with a spirit of enthusiasm, excitement and expectancy. I am at peace.

CPSIA information can be obtained at www.ICGtesting.com
Printed in the USA
LVOW101916200212

269567LV00001B/1/P